D0967039

Life After Youth

At the age of 35 she entered college; by 45 she had earned her Ph.D.; by 48 she was a tenured professor. The personal conviction and verve she brings to this book emphasize the possibilities open to older women who want to break out of stereotyped roles and fashion vital and interesting lives for themselves.

RUTH HARRIET JACOBS

Photo by Angela Kalovenpzos

LIFE AFTER YOUTH

Female, Forty – What Next?

Ruth Harriet Jacobs

BEACON PRESS
Boston

Library of Congress Cataloging in Publication Data
Jacobs, Ruth Harriet.
   Life after youth.
   Bibliography: p.
   Includes index.
   1. Middle aged women–United States. 2. Sex role.
   3. Aged women–United States–Social conditions.
   4. Aging–Psychological aspects. I. Title.
HQ1064.U5J3 1979   301.43'4   78-73854
ISBN   0-8070-3790-7

Acknowledgments

I would like to thank the National Institute of Mental Health for the grants R01 MH 26932 and R03 MH 22278 that funded some of the research for this book and the National Science Foundation for a postdoctoral fellowship to attend medical school in 1977-1978.

For the social concern to publish this book, I am grateful to Beacon Press and to my editors. Charlotte Cecil Raymond, though herself a young woman, understood the need for a book about older women. Her skillful encouragement helped me through the difficult hours of writing. I would also like to express my appreciation to Boston State College sociologist Frances Portnoy and psychiatrist Ruth M. Murphy of Lincoln, Massachusetts, for their careful reading of the manuscript and for their many insights. I also thank my typist, Ann Gratia C. Smith. The women who provided data and encouragement are too numerous to thank individually but I am grateful for their honesty and generosity.

To a marvelous young woman, my daughter, Edith Jane Jacobs, and my fine young female students, I dedicate this book in the hope that they will come into older womanhood in a time made happier for men and women everywhere by all our efforts.

Ruth Harriet Jacobs
Department of Sociology
Boston University

Contents

Introduction

ONE OF THE TASKS of sociology is to induce people to recognize inconvenient facts. This purpose was first stated by Max Weber, the keen German sociologist. Although he died in 1920, he predicted the Hitler era at a time when others were denying the possibility of such a calamity. Today many people, including some women, will not like to read the uncomfortable truth about the lives of older women. However, the facts I will discuss are the result of extensive research on the lives of aging women in the context of their options in American society, and they should be considered by anyone who hopes to change them.

Perhaps only a sociologist could write this book, for sociology, as C. Wright Mills pointed out, works at the juncture of biography and social structure. And, as people and social structures exist within historical periods, sociologists also understand that each individual is the child of the times as well as of parents and society. Often what are seen as individual troubles are really public issues. Sociology can thus be liberating; it can show people that what they consider their private crises or deficiencies may stem from public dilemmas. Individual troubles may be generated by societal difficulties, not by individual or group traits or behavior. Social structures and external events shape us and can create or block our opportunities.

Each *cohort*—people born at about the same time in the same society—shares an aggregate experience that forms its life to a large extent. To illustrate how individuals are thus affected, consider the experience of the cohort—American women born in 1924—to which I belong.

We arrived on earth in the shadow of Prohibition and the roar of the twenties that attempted to cover a tremendous post-World War I anxiety. Many of our parents were immigrants or the children of immigrants. Often they were "transitionals"—people who were rejecting their roots (before roots became acceptable and popular). Upward mobility and the emphasis on Americanization strained both our parents and us. As a result many of us grew up without consistent or clearly defined values.

For most of us childhood meant financial insecurity. In 1929, the Crash and the Great Depression that followed affected our four-year-old consciousnesses. Some of us were physically and emotionally severely deprived as our parents struggled and worried through those hard years. Sometimes they did not survive. Unlike the affluent adolescents we later spawned, we had no teen-age years of consumeristic pleasures. Suburbia and the indulgence and culture of adolescence were later creations. Families were less children-centered until we became parents and learned to give and give, even though we had not been given much in our own youth.

When we were in high school, economic conditions improved. Hitler invaded France when we were sixteen, accelerating an armaments race that ended the massive unemployment of the thirties. The Japanese bombing of Pearl Harbor brought America into the war in December 1941—our senior year in high school. Our boyfriends, or potential ones, went into the military. Though most of us would not have gone to college anyway—fewer women did so then—even fewer than usual went in 1942. We were needed to fill so-called men's jobs and do war work. Our brief experience with good pay and high responsibility showed us that we were capable of more than the traditional women's tasks.

Yet we were glad when the war was over and the men came home. Some veterans, however, selected brides from much younger cohorts, and some of us remained unmarried because the war casualties meant there were just not enough men to go around. Many who did marry bore children later than our mothers had and raised smaller families.

As housewives we had the benefit of technology developed during the war, but the household appliances and small families made us feel that we were less essential than our mothers had been. We knew we should be content to keep our modern new homes and children clean and our husbands happy, but we were vaguely discontented and felt guilty about it. Some of us yearned for the gratifications we had received during our working years.

After the war, society did not want us in the labor force. It was a classic case of ideology following economics. Despite the new domestic labor-saving devices, pediatrician Spock and other influential voices provided justification for full-time motherhood. The experts insisted that our children would be emotionally crippled if they did not receive 100 percent of their mothers' attention. So we were encouraged to hover in the nursery and kitchen. Our real function, however, was to be full-time consumers in a society of conspicuous consumption and overproduction. We were essential members of the affluent society.

By 1976, in a period of less affluence, the pendulum had swung the other way. Nearly half, 49 percent, of all mothers with children under 18 were in the labor force—compared with 35 percent in 1965, 27 percent in 1955, and only 9 percent in 1940. Now slightly over a quarter of all working mothers are between 25 and 34 years old, and about 5.1 million working mothers have children under six. But in the late forties and fifties women had successfully internalized the social sanctions against working mothers and were quick to criticize those with jobs and children. Women had been put in their place, the home, and they partly identified with the oppressor. In any case, the jobs available to women in the postwar period were clustered in the unattractive and poorly paid occupations (and they still are, despite propaganda and exceptions). It was hardly desirable or feasible for the middle-class woman of the 1924 cohort to be employed outside the home, especially as there was little good, available child care.

We swallowed, regurgitated, and performed the role of "supermom." We were very anxious about our children. After all, didn't more free time make it easier for us to create perfect children? Didn't the books tell us we could if we tried hard enough? Moreover, because we had electric servants, our husbands often felt we had it "too easy" compared to the competition they faced outside, so they left parental responsibility to us, even though they worked shorter hours than their fathers had. We even encouraged them to abdicate fathering, except for breadwinning; mothering was our one valued role, and we were jealous of it. The sexual division of labor became ingrained.

Our children were not perfect, in most cases. In the late sixties, our imperfect adolescents and young adults revolted against an imperfect society and against us—who had tried so hard to make them our friends. We had been permissive to encourage their autonomy and happiness, but they were dependent and unhappy. In the Vietnam era, they turned against authority, parental and otherwise, and experimented with drugs, violence, and sloth. At age forty-plus, we looked at our troubled products and felt like failures in the one important role society had allocated to us.

Most of us did not even blame our children for their attitudes and actions; "good mothers" to the last, our job was to excuse them and feel guilty. Blaming ourselves rather than children or society was painful, but at least the guilt orgy gave us a sense of importance. The surface self-blame was a defense against deeper feelings of impotence and loss. Who were we now that our children were grown, sometimes in strange ways? We were like the homeless bagladies who live in subways and public places, carrying their possessions in shopping bags. Our outgrown motherhood was burdensome, yet some of us clung to it and to our resentful adult children. If we were not mothers, we had no identity.

While we were mourning the loss or failure of our mother role, many of the 1924 and adjoining cohorts were also discarded as spouses. Encouraged by the media, some husbands blamed moms for the behavior and values of their progeny—as if children were entirely the product of women. Confused and themselves hurting, aging men berated or rejected their wives. Children, though disappointing, were after all their blood relations – whom their wives had corrupted. Their wives, those once desirable women, had failed them. Work, too, had often gone sour, and they wished they had spent more time with their sons and daughters, now strangers.

Their husbands' anger was a bitter pill to swallow, since these same men had earlier relegated child and adolescent care and worry to their wives and had done so cheerfully. Yet the 1924 women were so thoroughly conditioned to think of offspring as their exclusive responsibility that it never occurred to many of them to reject the blame. The failures were theirs alone – by a kind of immaculate self-deception – though they did not want to be reminded of them and punished for them by their husbands.

For these and many other reasons, sizable numbers of the 1924 female cohort found their marriages deteriorating or dead at a time when the omnipresent double standard classed them as past the age of sexual attractiveness. Their husbands' potency and egos were often insufficiently boosted by the latest model car, despite the hucksters. Daughter-aged women were bedded and wedded. The divorce rate for older marriages zoomed in the seventies, and most of the older women did not remarry. The men did – they married younger women.

The National Center for Health Statistics of the U.S. Census Bureau has estimated that the divorce rate more than doubled between 1963 and 1975: it rose from 2.3 per 1,000 population in 1963 to 4.8 percent in 1975. In 1976 in the United States there were 2.8 million men and 4.4 million women reported as divorced and not remarried. There were 75 divorced persons for every 1,000 persons who were partners in an intact marriage; the ratio was twice as high as the corresponding figure for 1960. Moreover, this ratio has risen more in the last six years than during the entire 1960-1970 decade, and many older marriages are among the casualties.

Even the happily married members of the 1924 cohort experienced problems. In their forties or fifties, they became aware of the women's movement message that they should be individuals with meaningful work and lives apart from their domestic role. Some rejected the idea and became defensively antifeminist. They felt faulted for what they had accomplished or suffered in good faith. The women's movement angered them because it made them feel inadequate or uncomfortable. Others embraced its ideology and wanted to feel strong and independent, but they felt weak and dependent because they had no marketable skills—or thought they hadn't. With children gone or growing up fast, they looked around for something worthwhile to do, but they couldn't type, key punch, or waitress fast enough—and that was all that was offered them. Consciousness-raising made many women discontented, but not all of them had any options, or felt they had.

Some of us were luckier; we were able to re-engage. In some ways, I was one of the lucky ones. After my children were in school, I got a bachelor's degree at 40, a Ph.D. at 45, and university tenure at age 48. Some of my personal experiences have influenced this book. But I have tried to empathize with older women who have had other kinds of lives. My informants for this book have come from all circumstances. I have conducted workshops on older women throughout the country and attended numerous professional meetings on the subject. I have listened to, interviewed, and observed older women in their homes and mine, their workplaces and mine, health clubs, beauty parlors, parties, hospitals and other medical settings, stores, restaurants, events, and meetings of all sorts—wherever older women gather. I have sometimes been delighted to see their strengths and the successes they have achieved despite great obstacles. However, I have also been distressed to hear of their frustrations and griefs.

In 1976 I prepared a typology of older women based on my sociological study of their lives and options. It happened that the editors of *Social Policy* magazine, knowing I had done research on the subject with support from the National Institute of Mental Health, asked me to write an article on re-employment in later life. Before agreeing, I looked over the projected table of contents for the special issue, "Older Persons: Unused Resources for Unmet Needs." I discovered there was to be no article on older women. When I mentioned this lack to the editors, they said they believed women had no special problems different from those of older persons in general. Still, they would be willing to consider such an article if I wrote it. I did. Its appearance in the November-December 1976 issue aroused much interest, and the requests for reprints amazed me. The experience encouraged me to write this book.

With some revisions, the typology that first appeared in *Social Policy* is used to organize this book. Each chapter discusses a different type of older woman: (1) nurturers, (2) unutilized nurturers, (3) re-engaged nurturers, (4) chum networkers and leisurists, (5) careerists—employed and unemployed, (6) seekers, (7) faded beauties, (8) doctorers, (9) escapists and isolates, and (10) advocates and assertive older women.

It is important to emphasize that no individual woman anywhere is described by any of these types. Rather the types are constructs for analytical purposes, attempts to understand the reality in order, perhaps, to change it. The real world and real people are, of course, so varied and complex that they could never be put into rigid little boxes. Clearly all of us have components of many of the types. We each juggle a unique package of different roles and statuses, and these change through our life-span. Experience brings growth, or should. Calamities cause dramatic shifts or stalemates. Adjustments occur.

Nonetheless, constructed types can give us a tool for examination—what is called a heuristic device. For most people at a given time one particular role is foremost. Other roles are on the "back burners," as physician Lewis Thomas wrote recently. What the typology can do then is to chart the roles that serve as paramount identifications for large numbers of older women. The types show the roles available to *most* older women today, not the roles they might like or would choose in an ideal world. Analyzing the types is a way to begin to understand what it is like to be an older woman today.

The roles people play affect them profoundly and are part of the web of social interaction. It is important to see how roles come to be developed and how they can be changed. If roles are dysfunctional—as many older women's roles are—how can we find more workable and comfortable roles for the better society all of us, men and women, deserve?

It was pointed out to me by Bernice Neugarten of the University of Chicago, past president of the Gerontological Society, that my typology of roles for older women can also be used to look at men's lives. However, the proportion of men and women of each type varies. For example, dramatically more women than men are predominantly nurturers, and more men are careerists. Realities and options are different for the sexes. Both men and women have to adjust to drastic life changes and often need emotional support and help in exploration. As sociologist George Herbert Mead said, we increase our repertoire of roles through life by incorporating those of significant others. We are not fixed forever in childhood patterns; we grow continually. That process is often facilitated by interaction with models and catalysts—counselors, friends, or heroes. As Albert Schweitzer said, "At times our light goes out and is rekindled by a spark from another person. Each of us has cause to think with deep gratitude of those who have lighted the flame within us."

I am grateful for the help, professional and personal, that guided me through some difficult role transitions, and I hope to reciprocate by helping others. Half of newborn Americans will be older women some day. We owe it to our daughters as well as to ourselves to work for better lives. And if women are unhappy, men's lives cannot be good. The women's movement has asserted all women are sisters, but, in addition, all girls of the future are our daughters and all boys our sons. We are connected through the generations. How we define and change our roles creates precedents for those who follow.

To redefine, however, we must first know what *is*, even if that knowledge hurts. The callous way Americans generally treat older women is a thermometer of a destructive fever afflicting our civilization. Dehumanizing part of the citizenry is a dangerous habit, for callousness can spread like a cancer. Who will be next? Once you label certain people as useless or bad, it is easy to consider them nonhuman and expendable, as was done in Vietnam and Nazi Germany. According to the same logic, some people over 70 are not resuscitated in some American hospitals; they are not considered worth saving.

What is so frightening to older women, and should be to society at large, is the fact that even gentle, unassuming older women easily become objects of undeserved hate, fear, and disgust. It is no accident that mythology pictures older women as witches and that poor old ladies were designated as witches and tortured throughout history. A disappointed or angry child can turn on its mother because it is usually safer to do so; father would return the hostility.

Later, unsure adult males, fearing the so-called female characteristics in themselves, project their self-doubt and hatred against women. The ambivalence they feel toward their mothers and their tendency to be hostile to women in general are kept somewhat in check toward young women by sexual and paternal self-interest and by men's pride in displaying young women as adornments. But older women, who are seldom the object of men's erotic fantasies or fathering impulses, can safely be made the scapegoats for past stresses endured in the parental household and present ones suffered in the larger society. Older women, like doting young mothers, are after all mostly defenseless and make excellent victims. Who defends them? Sadly enough, even young women often despise older women, seeing them as hourglasses in which to read, correctly, their own bitter fate.

The disdain and ridicule directed toward older women in the

United States is enormous. Treating them as nonpersons is so pervasive a cultural trait that often they even hate themselves and others of their age. As long as possible, many women deny, at least to themselves, that they are older women. When I told various older women I was writing a book to be called *Older Women in America*, they advised me to change the title. "Nobody will buy the book," they said. As the old joke goes, "An older woman is always someone twenty years older than you are."

The fact is that we *are* the older women–one in every five Americans. Nearing or past forty, we are no longer young, and most of us try to hide the fact from ourselves and other people. We are flattered when we are told that we don't look our age even though such "compliments" actually denigrate what we really are.

Yet, is it any wonder we accept such false compliments gratefully and deny and lie about our age? The double standard of aging labels women unattractive and obsolete at an age when men are seen to be at their most useful and distinguished. Yet women will outlive men by about eight years on the average (see Table 1). Life expectancy at birth is now 77 years for females and 69 years for males. Moreover, people who survive until later ages have an even greater than average life expectancy, as earlier deaths are included in these figures. In fact, at age 65, females on the average have 18 years left and males almost 14 years. At 70, males have approximately 11 years left and females approximately 14 years. At age 80 males have approximately 6 and females approximately 8 years left. Thus the longer you survive, the better your chances for a longer life. However, if you are a woman, you will find yourself in a world with fewer and fewer men. By age 65 there are 143 women for every 100 men.

We will be older women for more years than we were young ones. We have a long road to travel, but many of us do not know the way. The scarce maps we have are usually as outdated as our faces and bodies in a society that fetishizes youth. Some of us have rejected the life-styles of our mothers. Others are nostalgic for old

Table 1

U.S. Population over 30, by Age and Sex, 1976 (in thousands)

	TOTAL	MALE	FEMALE
30 to 34 years	14,238	7,045	7,193
30 years	2,895	1,442	1,453
31 years	2,796	1,386	1,410
32 years	2,854	1,409	1,445
33 years	2,993	1,479	1,515
34 years	2,699	1,329	1,370
35 to 39 years	11,916	5,819	6,097
35 years	2,537	1,246	1,291
36 years	2,401	1,174	1,228
37 years	2,365	1,152	1,212
38 years	2,339	1,139	1,200
39 years	2,275	1,108	1,167
40 to 44 years	11,160	5,451	5,708
40 years	2,260	1,101	1,159
41 years	2,240	1,096	1,144
42 years	2,201	1,075	1,125
43 years	2,232	1,089	1,143
44 years	2,228	1,090	1,137
45 to 49 years	11,662	5,678	5,983
50 to 54 years	11,981	5,759	6,222
55 to 59 years	10,754	5,132	5,622
60 to 64 years	9,310	4,355	4,956
65 to 69 years	8,281	3,662	4,619
70 to 74 years	5,913	2,505	3,408
75 to 79 years	4,051	1,586	2,465
80 to 84 years	2,724	982	1,742
85 years and over	1,966	629	1,337
Totals (Age 30 and above):	103,956	48,603	54,352

Source: Adapted from Bureau of Census, U.S. Dept. of Commerce, *Current Population Reports: Population Estimates and Projections*, Series P-643, January 1977, p. 7.

ways, though they are seldom possible today and were usually not so great anyway. Many of us thought the game was over when we

married and settled down, but it has begun anew when we are
tired, and the rules and roles have been changed. We thought we
would live out our lives as more-or-less happy wives and mothers.
Now we must struggle to survive, find new roles, and forget or
suppress the old rules.

Older women are underpaid, underutilized, underrecognized,
and underloved, even by ourselves. Although many consider us a
nuisance, we live on, sometimes painfully, sometimes joyously
and triumphantly, and–more likely as each year passes–alone
(see Table 2). Often we try to find new status and scripts in a
society that offers us few positive ones and makes jokes about our
struggles. Our options are limited, and the restrictive roles are
like ill-fitting shoes we wear because comfortable ones are not
available.

What is ironic is that although we are now a deprived minority, population trends make us the wave of the future. In 1950 the
average age in the United States was 20. In 1977 it was 28, and 50
years from now it will be 38 or 39. In the older age groups females
predominate because of their greater longevity. As Robert Benedict, new director of the federal Administration on Aging, said
in 1978 at Boston University: "There are enormous social impli-
cations in the fact that we are an aging society with women pre-

Table 2

Women's Marital Status after Age 35, 1976 (in percentages)

Status	35-39	40-44	45-54	55-64	64-74	75 and over
Single	5.2	4.2	4.4	4.9	5.9	6.0
Married, husband present	78.5	79.4	77.3	67.4	46.4	21.4
Married, husband absent (separated, in armed forces, other)	5.5	5.0	4.0	3.2	2.2	1.1
Widowed	1.9	3.2	7.2	19.1	42.0	69.7
Divorced (not remarried)	8.9	8.2	7.1	5.4	3.5	1.7

Source: Adapted from Bureau of Census, U.S. Dept. of Commerce, *Current Population Reports: Population Estimates and Projections*, Series P-20, no. 306, January 1977, p. 9.

dominating. We do not know what will be the effect of social relations and the impact on social security and pensions."

The women who are now older women are, therefore, the pioneers; the way society treats them will set a pattern for the future. What is worrisome is that a conservative trend and tax and national security concerns, plus prejudice, may prevent government officials and legislators from paying attention to older women's issues, which are already present and will soon be intensified by the rapid increase in women in this category. Commissioner Benedict believes that we "may be heading to a national calamity" because we are not preparing for an aging society. What is happening to older women now may be prognostic of this future disaster.

According to one well-established myth, women are now better off economically as a result of the women's rights movement. Yet a U.S. Department of Labor pamphlet, *The Earnings Gap Between Women and Men* (p. 1), reported that "women who worked at year-round full-time jobs in 1974 earned only 57 cents for every dollar earned by men. In fact, men's median weekly earnings exceeded women's by about $97 and women had to work nearly nine days to gross the same earnings men grossed in five days. . . . The earning differential is wider than it was nineteen years earlier." Since 1974 there has been a decline, not a gain, in women's relative position, and older women have usually fared the worst.

The situation for women heads of households is perhaps grimmest of all. The Department of Commerce, Bureau of Census reports in *A Statistical Portrait of Women in the U.S.* (p. 1) that "families headed by women were 13 percent of all American families in 1975. The proportion of families below the poverty level that are headed by women has increased, accounting for 46 percent of all families in poverty in 1974."

The median age of females in the United States has increased, from 22.4 in 1900 to 30 years in 1975, and it is expected to rise by another three to eight years by the year 2000, depending upon fertility rates. Older women are increasing and so is their poverty. A 1976 Department of Labor publication, *Mature Women Workers: A Profile*, estimated that 12.7 percent of all women 45 and over were living in poverty, though half of them worked. The figure for white women was 10.7 percent, and for minority women, it was 31.3 percent (of which 19 percent worked). The incidence of poverty increases with each decade, so that by age 65 and over, 18.3 percent of all women are living in poverty. By 65 and over, 40 percent of minority women are living in poverty.

There is real deprivation and consequent anxiety and anger for many older women. There is also the danger that critics, seeking reinforcement for their prejudices, will continue to believe that older women deserve their troubles. They claim that such women's unhappiness is a result of personality defects or unrealistic expectations instead of recognizing that many older women are unhappy because their essential human needs are unmet. Such persons see only symptoms and not their causes. They misperceive because they do not want to learn. They may even misinterpret this book as a criticism of older women instead of an explanation of how they are often pushed into unfortunate modes because of limited options. I hope this will not happen, for older women today need allies.

Jean Baker Miller has written insightfully of the results of inequality on women in her book, *Toward a New Psychology of Women*. When ageism is combined with sexism, older women are treated even less equally than younger women. Much older women are belittled by being called "little old ladies" or patronized as "cute"—a term for children. The rejection of middle-aged women is even less disguised.

Even those who do not care about the women themselves should realize that women, because of their longevity, cost the society economic and medical resources when they are not self-sufficient and healthy. Psychic pain turns physical, and health costs soar along with welfare budgets when older women have no useful, valued place in society.

Not many people espouse the cause of older women. In fact, older women often feel invisible, even though there are so many of them. When they speak, people tune them out. If they press to be heard or seen, they are called strident or pests. Should they complain when they are discriminated against or ignored, they are called resentful, cranky, hostile, and unfeminine.

There are only a few books and articles about older women; a handful of newsletters and networks have been organized by older women themselves. But the time has come when they must be acknowledged and helped. Either we must kill or destroy them all with neglect—and many do become addicted or suicidal, or ill in their despair—or we must listen.

In this book, I speak for myself and other older women, some of whom cannot or dare not articulate their complaints. I speak because I am a sociologist and a woman of 54.

CHAPTER ONE

Nurturers

AS PART OF OUR study of sex roles, I asked Laura, and her husband, Paul, to speak to my sociology class. Laura is fifty-five years old. Within the typology of roles for older women, she would be considered a nurturer – the motif most often assigned to older women both by themselves and by others. The undergraduates in the class found Laura's story unusual, but I saw her experience as rather typical of her agemates. Laura explains:

When I graduated from high school, where, like most of the girls, I took the commercial course, I got a secretarial job. Though as a child I loved to dance and looked forward to recitals where I starred, I never considered being a professional dancer. My folks would not have let me. Besides both they and I figured I would only work for a few years before becoming a homemaker.

At nineteen, I met Paul at a church dance, and we began to go steady. When he was drafted because of World War II, we got married. Fortunately he was not sent overseas but was based in the South, so I went there and made a little home for us until the war ended. When we came home, we moved in with my parents. As soon as the folks could get their tenants out of the other floor of their two-family house, we moved into that flat. We had our son, Jerry, soon and never had to have a babysitter because my mother always took care of him when we went out, which was not often anyway.

My father and Paul got along fine and often went to men's activities at the church or lodge together while Mom and I sewed, cooked, shopped, cleaned, or saw our friends to play bridge or whatever. Our son lived at home when he was going to college and until he got married.

When my dad got sick, my mother and I took care of him until the end, and he never, thank God, had to go to a hospital or nursing home. Then, because our neighborhood was running down, Mom sold the house. Paul and I bought a new one-family house in a better area, and Mom came to live with us. At first she helped with the housework and cooking and loved to garden in our nice new yard. Then she got sick, and for nearly five years I never left her unless I had someone reliable to come in and stay with her for a few hours. We never go on vacations anyway—we like our own home—so that was no problem. When Mom died, I was very sad and lonely. At first, I thought of getting a part-time job to keep busy and I even applied for one. They asked about recent experience. Then I decided that since I loved my home and Paul could support us, I could keep busy around the house.

What helped a lot was that my son's wife got pregnant shortly after mother died. It was exciting waiting for our grandchild. My daughter-in-law and son love to play tennis and go out to shows, so now Paul and I have steady babysitting at their house, which isn't far away. The baby is so cute and I love to buy things for her. I also like to cook stuff and bring it over there for them. I have a crib and high chair in my house.

Clearly Laura defines herself as a grandmother, mother, and wife. She says she feels content in the familiar circle of the family, although her life has little excitement by the standards of my students. In fact, she now recalls being a speaker in my class as a high point in her life.

Laura likes to listen to her husband talk about his job and loves going to company parties with him, planning her clothes carefully so he will be proud of her. She calls all his relatives, as well as her own, faithfully and never forgets birthdays or anniversaries. She has high blood pressure and sometimes her back hurts so that she feels tense and can't sleep. Otherwise, she reports, she is happy. She and Paul go to church every week and are active together in church organizations. If her physical complaints are of psychic origin—and this is hard to tell—she is unaware of it.

Laura's husband accompanied her to my class. She is fortunate, and knows it, for their relationship is close and loving, and Paul provides her with considerable companionship. Although not wealthy, the couple live very comfortably; Laura and Paul are home-centered people, and their recreations are inexpensive. Many couples like Laura and Paul report becoming closer after their children have grown up.

But other nurturers, women who have devoted themselves to home and children, do not enjoy companionship with husbands during later life. Among many American ethnic groups—and to some extent in the working class generally—there is a pattern of sharing recreational and social interactions with friends of the same sex rather than with spouses. This pattern was quite apparent during the great blizzard of 1978. Massachusetts was in a state of emergency, and all travel and business shut down. Every bar and coffee shop in one working-class, mostly Italian American, neighborhood was full of middle-aged and older men, sitting all day over coffee or beer. The wives, presumably, were at home or with women friends—certainly they were not with the men. As well-trained nurturers they might have fumed inwardly and burned the dinner, but they would not have berated their husbands for leaving them for most of the day. They expected it.

While the husband socializes on the job or hangs around at night or on weekends with "the guys," the wife often has social interaction with women relatives and neighbors. For women with small children, the necessity of mutual cooperation among neighborhood mothers fosters companionship. Women who work also share social activities with other women. Indeed many clerical workers who do not like the work itself enjoy getting out of the house "to be with people." For housewives and employees, the coffee klatch may be the high point of the day.

While a woman has young children, she may find her life quite busy, but when the interactions built around the children's needs and activities are no longer available, she may find a gap. As one forty-year-old woman told me: "Now every woman in the neighborhood is either younger than I am and busy with little kids or working. It's damn lonely and I know I chatter too much at my husband when he comes home. He turns the TV on to shut me out. I guess I'll have to do some volunteer work or something, if anyone will have me, or I'll go nuts. I don't feel needed. Joe is tired and doesn't want to go out at night. And on Saturdays he wants to go to the game with the guys."

The Nurturing Role

Nurturers have as their prime identity what has been called the traditional woman's role–the giving to others of food, love, and service. Sociologist Talcott Parsons calls this the *expressive* role, in contrast to men's *instrumental* roles. Nurturers' devotion to their husbands, children, and kin are their primary or most salient activity. Although they may also be employed outside the home, they think of their job as subsidiary to their roles as wives, homemakers, mothers, grandmothers, and mothers-in-law. Jean Baker Miller has pointed out that such women may feel guilty if they put their occupational or personal requirements above service in the domestic sphere. In addition, their employment often involves nurturant–and frequently exploitative–services, such as serving food, making the boss's coffee, teaching children, or nursing sick people. They listen to other people's troubles sympathetically, offer support, and consider this their job in life.

The learned predilection of nurturers is reinforced by the fact that others constantly define them in this role, no matter what other parts they try to play. It is a subtle process by which women, especially older women, are reminded that their family roles are seen as foremost. My personal experience is illustrative of this unconscious male mechanism. Last year when I was a National Science Foundation fellow at a prestigious medical school, nearly all the male physicians called me "Mrs. Jacobs." "Ruth" would have been fine, but if they wanted a title, "Professor Jacobs" or "Dr. Jacobs" would have been most appropriate since they called the male Ph.D.'s "Doctor." "Ms. Jacobs" would have been all right too. But "Mrs. Jacobs" was completely inappropriate as I am divorced, which they knew. Even older women who have never been married report that people insist on calling them "Mrs."

Are women thought to be flattered by being given the married title when they are past youth? Or is it that the status of older women, usually equated with the nurturance, overrides and blots out all other attributes and identifications? Is it that people don't see us as individuals? Do they just see our age and ascribe to us the status they think is appropriate—that of nurturers? Is it any wonder that long-term nurturers find it difficult to move into any other status—in actuality as well as in their own consciousness?

Relatively few older women have been given the early socialization or education that would equip them for activities other than nurturing. The jobs Laura could have obtained with her rusty secretarial skills would have been tedious. Moreover, her volunteer work was done at home, in faithful care of her parents after her child grew up. These duties took up so much of her time that she never really developed outside interests. Under these circumstances it was natural for her to turn, as an older woman, to the marital bond as the principal source of affection and stimulation.

For many nurturers like Laura the best friend *is* the spouse, and other relationships are subsidiary. This is why women who have had the closest marriages are so devastated when their husbands die; all their emotions are invested in one person.

Of course, not all women's needs are met so well in the marriage relationship. Many married older women who may seem to be content nurturers are in truth quite desperate—homemaking activities being insufficiently fulfilling. Some have outgrown or grown apart from their husbands, yet they maintain the façade of the happy housewife. Others are neglected by busy or otherwise emotionally involved husbands. The effort required to suppress or repress their discontent is costly and often results in chronic de-

pression. Yet they are immobilized; they cannot change because
feminist rhetoric has not reached their inner core—that deeply
imbedded notion that they should be content with their nurturing
role. Even though nurturing is just not enough for them in their
older years, they do not know how to extricate themselves from its
constraints. In fact some women, in their desperation to continue
nurturance, irritate adult children by asking them repeatedly,
"Would you like something to eat"—as if this were their only form
of communication or caring expression. Some of these adult offspring, fighting the great American war on calories, blame their
mothers for overfeeding them as children and creating what are
popularly called "greedy fat cells." Such children look resentfully
at pictures of themselves as plump babies and berate their
mothers. It is no wonder that some mothers feel victimized and
resentful for what they did in all innocence in an era when calen-
dars and baby books showed fat babies as the norm. Other
mothers take upon their drooping shoulders the burden of their
progeny's adult obesity when the children's own greed is as much
if not more at fault.

Nurturing traits indeed endure. One forty-year-old professional reports that her mother still asks if she has remembered to
go to the bathroom before leaving for the long ride home after a
visit. Such women are trying to be useful in the only way they
know. Other "retired" mothers depend on activities with women
friends for outlets; these women, the chum networkers, will be
discussed in a later chapter. Others may become doctorers.

Laura is very lucky that her daughter-in-law loves her and is
willing to share her grandchild. Some grandmothers are thwarted
in their desire to continue in the nurturant role. Geography or the
rejecting of children or grandchildren deprive them of such expression. In addition, many young couples today are deciding not
to have children or are postponing them—to the consternation of
would-be grandmothers.

Actually, few older nurturers are as outwardly happy in their
roles as Laura. Many feel that their own lives have been squeezed

between the needy young and the greedy old or between the greedy young and the needy old. Many mid-life women complain that they have never had the time or money to fulfill their own needs because they have had to take care of their children. Then, just when their children reach college and expenses mount, aging parents begin to need time, emotional support, and, in some cases, financial help. Mothers finish taking care of pediatric diseases and emergencies only to be confronted with geriatric diseases and emergencies. As social worker Elaine Brody of the Philadelphia Geriatric Institute noted, one daughter, frequently the oldest, becomes "the burden bearer"; her empty nest is filled. Not all burden bearers, however, can accept this extra responsibility as cheerfully as Laura, and many couples, unlike Laura and Paul, have more than one child to worry about and send through college. Mid-life women dealing with the rebellions and expenses of a number of college young sometimes feel they do not have enough energy and sympathy left for ailing parents or husbands suffering through a career or health crisis.

Nurturers, like most other Americans, frequently fear that their own old age will be difficult and sad. Watching their parents struggling to cope with old age, they wonder when, and whether, they will finally get their reward for all their hard work. Secretly all nurturers probably hope someone will notice and reward them.

Overextended nurturers, the burden bearers, who break down and ask for help from physicians usually get Valium or Librium instead of a solution to their problems. Yet however easy it is to join the criticism of physicians for making these women addicts, it is clear that some problems are insoluble, given the values and arrangements of this society. In most areas there is simply no support for those who must care for the young and the old. Day care for the elderly hardly exists, and in its absence most faithful daughters are rightfully reluctant to commit their frail, aged parents to profitmaking nursing homes. Temporary care of elderly people, so that burden bearers may vacation, is also rare.

Such arrangements are possible, however, as one Chicago Jewish community has demonstrated by supporting a short-term residence for elders.

It is ironic that the very women who never felt free to leave their children will probably have few free years before they take on the responsibility for aging parents, even as they age themselves.

Robert Benedict, the director of the federal Administration on Aging, announced in 1978 that the new approach of the agency will be "to return the responsibility for the aged to families." Mounting nursing home costs and the scandals associated with many homes were, of course, behind the announcement. Nonetheless, there were no signs that the agency planned sizable efforts to aid the families who were supposed to help the aged. When I asked Benedict about this he said he recognized that few families neglect their old, despite the media's contentions. He wishes to eliminate what he considers "dis-incentives" to families who would like to care for their old people at home. Knowing that many women must work and cannot care for aging parents, Benedict also recognizes that the mood in the country favors retrenchment, not increases in social services. If the trend continues, he feels there is a real danger to the old and those who are their caretakers.

Economics and Liberation in the Home

Another factor that makes life difficult for older nurturers is the menial, low-paying, low-satisfaction jobs they are forced to take because their husbands' salaries cannot cover inflationary prices or because they have lost their husbands through death, divorce, or desertion. When a woman believes her chief role is to be available to the family, going to work out of economic necessity puts her into conflict with herself. She tries desperately to keep up her standards of homemaking and caring for her family while her energy is drained by hard, ungratifying work. As she gets older, it becomes even more tiring to balance the demands of home and an uncongenial job, especially for a poorer woman who lacks the attractive jobs and good health care available to her better-educated, more mobile upper- or middle-class sisters.

If a waitress or cashier who is an older woman looks exhausted and is a bit slow, consider that before she came to work at 7:00 A.M., she may have packed her husband's lunch, ironed his shirt and her uniform, made the beds, and done the breakfast dishes. She will hurry home after work, stopping at the grocery to make sure her husband has a good, homemade dinner. On her day off she will do the big shopping, laundry, and heavy housework, and on Sunday she will cook a dinner for her grown-up kids. When they leave early to go back to college and "study for exams," she will do the dishes alone. Once in a while, when she is sick or at the end of her rope, her husband will help with "her" work and expect her to be grateful. He is not a bad person; he simply shares her assumption that the home is her province even though she works outside.

Certain readers may come to the conclusion that the lady just described is living in the dark ages. They may be dark, but they still exist—even for the new breed of nurturer—as I was surprised to learn when I attended a NOW-sponsored workshop last year. I was one of only two women past forty at the meeting. The other twenty were around thirty, and most of them were married; many had careers and most had children. They described their efforts to live as "liberated women" and to have egalitarian marriages. They found that they could do neither.

These young married women were just as much in the nurturance trap as women of their age were thirty years ago. They did most of the housework and took most of the responsibility for buying and preparing the food. Sometimes husbands helped them with "their chores," but both the men and the women saw care of the home and children as essentially women's work. As the other older woman and I left the meeting we agreed that it was as if the women's movement had never happened. These college-educated, bright, working women still saw themselves as nurturers first, and their men cooperated to let them carry almost the entire responsibility for their homes. Some of them looked tired and strained, and I do not think they were unrepresentative. Most married female interns, residents, and physicians carry the primary responsibility for the home too, and they are always tired. Is there a relationship between this fact and their high divorce rate?

Women graduate students still amost always type their husbands' papers and do the cooking and cleaning. Then they wonder why the better jobs and fellowships go to the men, who have more time to socialize in the department and write. The standard joke among women law students is that a man needs a wife to do his mundane work. It is the same story among business and academic women who sometimes cannot help feeling envious of the dozens of little personal services provided to male colleagues by their wives.

Yet even the young women who would like to reject the nurturance model provided by their mothers often find it hard to do so. Questions and guilt nag them. Instead they end up hating themselves, their mothers, and all older women for being what young women would rather not become.

The Dangers of Nurturance

Nurturing is a good human activity. Mutual nurturance is needed by both men and women of all ages, but one-sided nurturance can become as addictive as sugar, tobacco, alcohol, or heroin. And in excess it can be just as dangerous. Though caught by it, the addict may hate the source of his addiction. Consider the situation of a man whose ego and well-being rest on the slavish devotion of a woman who puts his needs at the center of her life—above her own. The more care she delivers, the more he demands, to test his power and assuage his guilt. She must deliver her services promptly in order to assure him that his demands and expectations are proper and that she will remain always the giver, he the given. Aging, and feeling weak and frustrated in the outside, often unfriendly world, more and more he turns to the nurturer to give him what he has not found elsewhere. Especially if he is blocked in his career, she must be the perfect mother, more perfect than the real one who–after all–let him go and perhaps disappointed him.

It may be the nurturers who are most often the victims of wife beaters. Such women take upon their bodies the hatred of their men, living, sometimes for years, in fear. Somehow they feel bound to accept this role: "He couldn't help himself," they say. Only now has the support offered by other women through ideology, sanctuaries, and other avenues encouraged some battered wives to stop offering this ultimate service as receptacles of their husbands' anger and frustration.

It may also be true that wife beating has increased, in addition to getting more publicity. Alienation is a cliché, but it is a truth in our society. Many men, frustrated in their work lives or unemployed, find the final straw to be that their wives want something more from life than the opportunity to serve them. As midlife women finish their childrearing years and feel free to grow, they reach out and find support from the mass media and other women. They become re-educated. That the drug of nurture might be diminished for the addicted man fills him with fear and hate. In our aging-phobic society, he already half hates his older wife because her aging proves that he is no longer young. If she seeks and finds new adequacy when he is feeling inadequate, he is enraged. The fact that older women may now have more time to read and become articulate may threaten aging men whose jobs make them feel harried and insecure. Sometimes, he grows too. But sometimes he insults or beats her until she leaves him, or he leaves her, seeking a more pliable, inexhaustible nurturer.

The June 26, 1978, issue of the *Women Today* newsletter, published in Washington, D.C., carried the following report:

The American home may not be a haven of warmth and security but rather a curtain hiding a great deal of violence, particularly physical abuse of women by husbands and boyfriends, concluded anthropologist Dr. Sabra F. Woolley of Washington, D.C. Woolley's extensive research is reported in "Battered Women: A Summary," published recently by the Women's Equity Action League (WEAL). Woolley states that as many as 50 percent of the women living with men are subject to physical abuse. Such abuse ranges from a slap in the face to life-threatening beatings or attacks with weapons. Reasons are often as trivial, Woolley says, as having forgotten to put lettuce in a sandwich.

The woman who is nurtured by a man can nurture him well. But unreciprocated nurturing often leads to exhaustion or a despising and despised spouse. Building a life around nurturance has other pitfalls as well. In our society, older women nurturers have a high rate of obsolescence, as we shall see in the next chapter.

CHAPTER TWO

Unutilized Nurturers

HERE IS A TRUE story about a nurturer who is suddenly without someone to nurture:

Deborah, clogged with her cold, plowed through the March wind, cursing the dog excreta and glass fragments littering the city where she had lived for a year since her divorce from Harry and suburbia. She had been born in this city forty-five years ago; it had deteriorated since her childhood. She pulled her hood down to avoid the cheerful hellos of young couples who inhabited the apartments around her and to hide the painful sight of old Miss Green, the retired schoolteacher, walking, as always, alone.

Deborah found it hard to move fast enough to avoid encounters because she had accumulated seventy extra pounds. She had begun to gain as she contemplated and carried out the divorce. Afterward, living alone and repressing her anger and depression to present a cheerful front to the world, she continued to overeat. After reviewing the history of her twenty-five-year marriage, her attorney had told her she had the right to be angry. But that lawyer could not tell her a good way to express the anger and disappointment that drove her out into this windy, cold day to buy a loaf of bread, which she would consume without really tasting it. It would give her some momentary relief and stupefy her so she would not feel so keenly the loss of the accustomed family setting.

This weekend, because of her cold, she had not made any plans, though she usually went away from the apartment. She had intended to stay home to rest and clean. Besides she was tired of the other unhappy or frenetic women with whom she spent her weekends. She felt sickened when they talked of their sexual needs or affairs. Their wants reminded her of her own; their solutions dismayed her. She had avoided seeing one acquaintance again after she told her she found lovers among newly divorced and widowed men by using the obituary column and other sources.

Her married friends, of course, were busy with their spouses, and they had stopped inviting her to parties where all the other guests were coupled. She envied them for not being losers. When she first moved into her new apartment Deborah had held a dinner party for some of these married friends. One brought her towels monogrammed with Deborah's first initial, because "it seemed safer." Why did she have to rub it in? Was any monogram needed? That night, when the couples had gone home together, she felt lonelier than ever.

Last night she had felt so cooped up in the small apartment that she had gone to a hotel for dinner. After eating too much, she had been unable to face her empty apartment and had sat in the hotel lobby. She watched while a couple about her own age came out of the dining room. The man told the woman to wait while he got the car; then he brought the car, collected the woman, and tenderly tucked her in. Deborah didn't want to sit there any longer, but she could not bear to go home, so she decided to go to the top floor of the hotel to look at the view. Riding the elevator, she considered throwing herself off the roof, but she knew she would never act on her fantasy because she could not hurt her children.

Like everything else lately, the view was disappointing, and she quickly re-entered the elevator. Several floors down, an attractive man about forty-five, her age, entered, said hello, and asked where she was from. When she replied that she was from that city, he asked "What is going on here?" Although she answered "Nothing" rather curtly, he persevered: "I'm here on business for several weeks. Will you have dinner with me?" She answered no, but when they left the elevator he followed her through the lobby, begging her to have dinner another night or to give him her phone number. She thought "He probably thinks I'm an overage call girl" and fled. Lying to him and to herself she called, "I have to go home to my husband." She was frightened, although he seemed nice. She was scared that he wanted her, that the fat was no longer protection.

She was shaking. She knew that she had hung around that hotel unconsciously hoping that someone would notice her. Once noticed, however, she had been unable to handle the encounter. She had once heard a speaker say that he could tell almost immediately after the death of the husband whether a widow would be likely to remarry. Perhaps she, like widows who continued to mourn, would never be available for intimacy again; she still had too much invested in what had failed. In blurting out "I'm going home to my husband" she had mouthed her fantasy. She was scared at how easy it would have been to have dinner and sleep with the stranger, and she understood now the friends whose affairs she despised.

Deborah had spent some time analyzing her divorce. She realized that she had gone through three stages. First there was pride and triumph that she had successfully made a move that had to be made. She was able to leave Harry's house and set up her own place, and she felt alive and self-reliant. Then she had gone through a period of grief and depression. The house was lost, the role was gone, and the hopes that Harry would change were finally destroyed. And now, she had come to compensation; she was compensating all over the place, but she was still unhappy. This morning, after the hotel experience, she was going out for bread, although she had promised herself to eat only soup, salad, and a protein supplement today.

Having bought bread and frozen orange juice, Deborah passed a clothing shop with a sale sign and went in to kill time. She looked through racks; nothing seemed big enough. It was difficult to know what size she wore; she had gained weight so steadily that she scarcely recognized her own body. Last week she had dreamed of seeing a woman in a tent dress like one she had bought recently; in the dream Deborah had asked, "Who is that stranger?"

Deborah scanned the flannel nightgowns, looking for one

large enough to provide comfort in the cold apartment. She selected two that seemed possibilities and went into the fitting room, but they were too small. When she asked the hovering proprietor to find her a larger size, the woman returned with a bright-red, satin, sleeveless monstrosity complete with low neckline and cheap black lace hearts.

"You look unhappy," the woman explained, "I don't want you to go away frustrated. We have to help each other. This will fit, and you can have it half price, six dollars."

To be obliging, Deborah tried it on and indeed it did fit, making her look like an oversize whore. (She recalled the previous night's encounter.) It was obviously left over from Valentine's Day — it was the kind of gown a man would buy for his lover and that no woman would buy for herself, except a desperate one "on the make." It was sleazy and would have to be hand washed, but it would still run and rip. Deborah knew the "bargain" price was a way to get rid of obsolete merchandise, but she also understood that the other woman saw her pain — her face showed real concern. Looking in the mirror Deborah knew why; her hair was unkempt and her eyes and mouth reflected loneliness. So in the psuedo-intimacy of the tiny fitting room Deborah, who was usually so self-possessed, broke into tears and said, "You are right. I am unhappy; I got divorced recently after twenty-five years."

The woman blurted "Why?" and Deborah answered "because he wanted to stay young." She knew this wasn't entirely true, life and interactions always being exceedingly complex. But she felt rejected by Harry and by life, and anger spilled like the unwanted tears. The saleslady, too, responded with anger, "I hear of many such cases. I hope the young hussy gives him what he deserves."

Feeling a naked fraud, dramatic, Deborah escaped quickly with the nightgown, thanking the owner for "the bargain" she didn't really want. "I hope it gives you good luck," the woman said. Like Deborah's acquaintances, she was speculating on how long she would take to get a man. Tina at the office had said that the secretaries were "making book" that number two would be terrific. Deborah herself felt sure she would spend a lonely old age.

She took the nightgown home and buried it in the back of her closet where her daughter would not see it when visiting. Once, during the holiday season, she had gone out to dinner with her daughter, a bright, independent twenty-two-year-old. Deborah, slightly drunk, felt a terrible longing to dance to the marvelous band. She had said to her daughter: "Would you be shocked if I went out some time with a man, so I could dance?" Her daughter had replied, "I wouldn't be shocked at *anything* you did with a man," thus giving her subtle permission. Still, Deborah hid the nightgown from her daughter and herself, though she did not throw it away.

She ate some of the bread, put on a shabby old nightgown and got into bed. Her cold felt worse after the walk and shopping. She felt even more depressed than usual and was too tired to vacuum. She was angry at herself for being greedy, knowing she was much luckier than many divorced women; at least she had a job and a fairly decent salary.

She turned on the television set, but it bored her. Finally she got out of bed and went to the kitchen and got the vodka down from the high shelf where she kept it. She usually drank only with guests, but as she took it down, she realized she had bought the frozen orange juice, perhaps planning unconsciously to drink a screwdriver. She started to sob hysterically because she could not bear to think of herself as coming to this—so helpless that she must drink alone as well as overeat. She wanted to be strong. She wanted to conquer this pain. She thought, "I'll feel better when the cold is gone; I'll feel better in time." She went back to bed without the drink and tried to read, but her eyes teared. In an hour, she returned to the kitchen and mixed a double jigger of vodka with the orange juice, drinking it in two minutes. This and a boring television program soon put her to sleep.

When she awoke the next morning, she remembered that she had not fed her plants for months. They had come from her old home; she had brought them here the day before she moved so there would be something to welcome her. She sprayed the leaves, thinking "I'm sublimating." One plant had cost her fifty cents at a garage sale; it was so scrawny no one had wanted it. Deborah had said, "It needs a home; I'll adopt it."

Deborah felt *she* was now a neglected plant but was disgusted with herself for wanting someone, a man, to take care of her. She also wanted someone to take care of. All she had learned in the women's movement about self-sufficiency warred with her early training, with her need for intimacy – for nurturing and being nurtured. Un-nurtured now and un-nurturing, she felt empty.

Sometimes when her adult children came to visit her, she wanted desperately to touch them or to have them touch her. A few times she had kissed them, but they had stiffened and brushed her away, as they had when they were five. Deborah remembered how much she had hated it when Grandma, who had lived alone, fondled her. Now, with Gram long dead, she knew how hungry for a human touch the old lady must have been.

Deborah tenderly potted an overgrown cutting that had been hanging around for months. As she did so, she thought: "My roots are constricted too. My life has no place to expand." Putting the new plant on the window sill, she noticed a bird on a branch outside. She looked at the bird and the tree instead of at the overflowing garbage and the broken bottles in the alley. She thought, "The tree will leaf out soon and hide the mess." She smiled, recalling that she had not thrown away the nightgown and wondering whether she would take it along on her summer vacation. She began to fantasize about meeting an eligible man whom she could have to the apartment for dinners. She would fix up the apartment and lose weight to make him proud of her.

As Deborah had her coffee, she thought: "It has taken the cutting time to heal and grow roots. Maybe I need time, too. Maybe I need more patience with myself. Maybe someone will turn up."

Her cold seemed better. She put the vodka back on the high shelf.

One of today's many older divorcées, Deborah is mourning her lost roles and having difficulty finding satisfactory new ones. Not all divorcées, widows, and empty nesters resent their current condition, however. Some enjoy the freedom of not having to take care of others. Many are happy in their new situations, and some even undergo a renaissance. They keep occupied with new interests and find within themselves unknown abilities and the determination to develop latent skills.

Deborah, however, is unhappy and pins her hopes on the appearance of a new man to nurture. But the population statistics are against her, for there are fewer older men than older women because of the differences in mortality; with every decade of age the sex ratio becomes more and more disparate until, after 65, there are only 69 men for every 100 women. At Deborah's age, 45, there are 92 men for every 100 women. And, alas, the older men who do survive generally prefer younger women. It might be that if Deborah lost weight her chances would improve. On the other hand, singles' clubs, bars, and resorts are already overpopulated with slim, attractive older women who are alone or with other females.

Deborah's faith that she will find another man is quite consistent with female indoctrination. Such legends as Sleeping Beauty and Rapunzel letting down her hair to harvest a lover deeply affected us. If the fairy tales did not get to us, Hollywood and television and romantic literature conditioned us to believe that "someday my prince will come."

Deborah was also not unique in her experience of being abandoned by married friends after her divorce. With variations, the Deborah story is related by many women excluded by the convention of pairing. One put it this way: "Do they think that because we are divorced, we are going to rape their husbands and break up their families?"

The Noah's ark syndrome, two by two, is so deeply embedded in middle-aged and older persons that only the rare liberated hostess will invite a single woman without a male partner. In fact, one happily married older woman tells the following story, which is not unusual, bizarre as it seems. "My husband and I were invited to dinner at our good friends, the Smiths. There were to be four other couples there, all of whom are part of our crowd. The day of the party, my husband came down with a terrible cold; so I called Betty Smith and told her I would be coming alone. I figured she would cook less and set one less place. That evening she met me at the door, terribly apologetic, to say that she had phoned around all day but just couldn't find a dinner partner for me. Why did I need a man to have dinner?" It apparently never occurred to the hostess that an unaccompanied adult woman was an acceptable guest, as certainly only gastronomic orgies were planned!

Many single people have a scanty social life, although things are improving slightly now that there are so many unattached persons. Among younger people, it is acceptable to be uncoupled, but older generations are often stuck with their early conditioning. Clearly Deborah finds it hard to accept her single state. She feels a failure without a man, even though she is not willing to settle for pick-ups or casual experiences.

Deborah, like many divorced women, has lost more than a husband. Formerly marrieds report that even unhappy marriages provided a feeling of belonging in society. Growing up in an era when there was still a stigma attached to divorce, they find that though society has changed, many people of their generation have not. For example, one 53-year-old divorcée of two years tells new acquaintances that she lost her husband so that they will feel sorry for her instead of asking themselves what was wrong with her that she couldn't sustain a marriage.

Others feel the loss of in-laws after their marriage ends. One woman was outraged when her former mother-in-law had a heart attack and nobody called her. "I should have been at the hospital," she insisted. After a divorce, nurturers often lose a whole network of giving and receiving relationships they had depended on. Though the relationships may have been difficult, they at least sewed the woman into the garment of social interaction. Without them, they feel naked. Widows too are occasionally cut off from the spouses' kin, but this tends to happen less often, less abruptly, and with less acrimony.

Deborah does have grown-up children in her life and may be envied by older woman who are completely alone. But good nurturer that she is, she wants to avoid imposing on her children. She keeps a happy face before them, chatters about her "busy life," and wants them to be free of her needs. She is smart as well as generous to do this, for complaining or clinging would almost surely drive them away.

Displaced Homemakers

Deborah knows that she is fortunate to have a job. Many so-called displaced homemakers are suffering economically because they cannot compete for scarce entry-level jobs with their more nubile and better-educated daughters. Women who stayed home for many years to raise children have much knowledge and experience, but it is not always easily marketable. They also have wrinkles.

In California, Tish Sommers and others of the NOW Older Women's Task Force were instrumental in getting the state legislature to pass the Displaced Homemakers' law, which provides for retraining of such women. Other states have followed suit and there is now a similar federal program included in CETA, the Comprehensive Employment Training Act. The troubles of ex-nurturers were cogently explained in a paper published by the Alliance for Displaced Homemakers (ADH):

> These are women who have fulfilled a role as a homemaker, who find themselves "displaced" in their middle years, through divorce, widowhood or other loss of family income. They are ineligible for AFDC if their children are over 18. They are subject to the highest

unemployment rate of any sector of the work force. They face discrimination in employment because they are women, older and have no recent paid work experience. They are ineligible for unemployment insurance because they have been engaged in unpaid labor in the home. They are ineligible for Social Security because they are too young. Some will never be eligible because they are divorced and fall through the cracks of the S.S. system. Many lose medical coverage and are unacceptable for private health insurance plans.

An exact figure is hard to find, because homemakers don't often appear in government statistics. Since their economic contribution is not recognized, and they receive no benefits, their status is officially ignored. Rough estimates on the number who fit the description are 1 to 3 million.

The changing status of the family has caught older women unprotected. The divorce rate has doubled. There has been an increase of 46 percent in the number of households headed by women in ten years. One fourth of the divorces filed are after more than 15 years of marriage. The trend is toward no-fault dissolution of marriage and spousal support for limited periods, if at all. Increasing numbers of older women live without men. There are more than four times as many widows as widowers. The older women become, the more likely they are to be on their own.

The ADH has now disbanded, but its leaders are active in behalf of displaced women in the Older Women's League Educational Fund, which was founded in 1978. This organization's first large-scale action was a national training conference on displaced homemakers held in Baltimore, Maryland, in October 1978. The conference was made possible through a grant from ACTION and was presented with the cooperation of the Women's Bureau of the Department of Labor.

The federal government is indeed concerned about displaced mid-life women, perhaps for financial rather than humanitarian considerations. After all, if they are unable to care for themselves, such women will end up on federal welfare roles. (They are also voters, of course, and there are a lot of them.) In 1978 the House of

Representatives Select Committee on Aging, headed by Representative Claude Pepper, commissioned a report and asked for recommendations on American women in mid-life. The report is scheduled for 1979 publication.

When Robert Benedict, director of the Administration on Aging, was asked at a June 1978 public meeting in Boston what efforts were being made to provide funds for widows below the age of 60 and for other older women not entitled to social security, he replied that he knew of no such efforts. He pointed out that the concern about older women's plight is surfacing just as the country seems most adverse to making social investments because the economy is no longer expanding and resources are limited. The director added: "I can't think of a worse time in our history to be moving to an aging society."

Nobody knows exactly how many women, many of them ex-nurturers, fall through the cracks of the system of pensions and social security. Some who are entitled to benefits do not get them because they do not know how to cope with the system. So if you see older women pocketing rolls in a restaurant or grocery do not assume that they are eccentric. They may be hungry; their aid (if they have any) may be exhausted this month. There are almost no sources of help for such women. Here is an example of one such woman:

Sylvia had been married for 35 years when, one day last year, her husband took off. She doesn't know where he is. She is 55 and thus is not eligible for the hot lunch provided under the nutrition program of the Older Americans' Act. Yet she looks older than her age, so she goes, with considerable embarrassment, to her local church hot lunch. One well-meaning but naive sociology student observing her there asked, "You come here for the sociability, to see people, don't you?" Sylvia told him she came to see food. The student noticed that she ate all the hot food, but put the piece of fruit and a slice of bread into her pocketbook. "That's my supper," she explained. "What do you have for breakfast?" the young man asked. Sylvia smiled. "Oatmeal. I have no way to cook in my room so I have an oatmeal cookie."

Sylvia is at least able to get to one hot meal a day; some older women cannot. Dr. Frances Portnoy, who did a magnificent survey of older persons for the Newton, Massachusetts, Department of Public Health, found that there were undernourished older persons even in that affluent city. She also found many isolated, lonely people.

Older women have the lowest average income of any group in America; older black women are in the very worst economic situation. Some older women living alone in single rooms, as many do, have no cooking facilities and eat very badly. Some are near starvation or subsist on cheap starches. Some have become poor late in life after loss of spouse or employment and have never had a chance to learn how to survive on a low income. More than 21 percent of American households consist of a single person, many of whom are former nurturers.

There are, of course, levels of suffering. Former nurturers, like Deborah, who are employed at skilled work do not starve like Sylvia, but they often do suffer loneliness, self-denigration, and fear of failure. Their distress can have severe outcomes. Deborah fantasized suicide but did not act. Others do.

Nurturers displaced by divorce are a high-risk group for suicide, according to Sonya J. Herman of the American Association of Suicidology: "Suddenly the woman must live for herself and give up the old role of existing for others."

Help for Ex-Nurturers

Living alone for the first time in her life, Deborah was, as we saw, working alone to overcome her depression. Many other women in her situation turn to other people for help. Often they seek out paid counselors to help them identify with their new roles, but not all of them are fortunate in their choices. In most states, anyone can hang out a shingle or advertise as a "counselor." Sadly many incompetent therapists and even charlatans are trading in on the older woman's need to be nurtured, guided, and relieved of unnecessary guilt and repressed rage. Some so-called feminist therapists have as their only credential the fact that they have survived their own crises. Although most mean well, their individual and group therapy is not always helpful and may in fact add to the difficulties of older women who need skilled help.

The story of two women who offered group therapy for "transitional women" is a case in point. Both leaders were in their thirties. One had a B.A. in French literature and had taught high school briefly before leaving to raise a family. The other had small children, needed money, and had a B.A. in psychology. They enrolled twelve mid-life women, at a large fee, for eight sessions held at a community center. At the third session, the leaders singled out a woman of about forty who seemed depressed and had not yet spoken much. They asked her, in front of the group, a series of probing questions that an experienced therapist would have spread out over months so as not to arouse too much anxiety. For a while the woman answered frankly, if hesitantly, but then said she felt uncomfortable; she had said more than she wanted to in front of the group and was feeling exposed and upset. At this point, the first hour was up. The leaders declared the usual recess to run out and put dimes in parking meters. The confronted woman, instead of putting a dime in the meter, got into her car. When one of the leaders noticed and ran over to ask why she was leaving, the woman repeated that she was very upset and had not wanted to share her feelings so much with the group. The leader told her that leaving would destroy the group rapport, and stated that it was very selfish of her to do so. She promised that if the woman returned she would not be spotlighted further. The appeal to her nurturance hit home; not wanting to upset the group she came back.

However, the leader began with: "Sally doesn't want to talk anymore, but I feel uncomfortable about this. I think she should. How does the group feel?" A few people sat dumbfounded, but the rest backed up the leader. The leaders again confronted the depressed lady, badgering her for an hour while the group watched.

By the end of the hour, she was crying and very disturbed. They then just let her go.

Though Sally had paid her money for all of them, it is not surprising that she did not show up for the last five sessions. What is surprising is that neither leader had the concern, sense, or courtesy to phone her to see what happened. They neither sent her a refund nor, apparently, realized that they had any responsibility for upsetting her.

Later two women from the group did call the victim to ask how she was. They found her more depressed than ever because she had wasted her money. She blamed herself for talking and exposing herself; as nurturers often do, she was directing her anger inward instead of against her oppressors. For a long time she had difficulty dealing with the feelings evoked by that vigorous and injudicious confrontation.

Sadly, incidents of this sort are not rare. People feeding their egos and pocketbooks abound in the therapy business. Nevertheless, transitional women often do get genuine aid and support from various types of groups, including self-help and support groups in which women with common problems exercise judgment and tact in dealing with each other.

There are also referral services, especially in urban areas, to direct such "walking wounded," the hurting ex-nurturers. However, such services vary in their quality, as do therapists, and trustworthy referral is absolutely essential. Some of the women who most need help do not know where to get it. As one displaced housewife said: "I'm as displaced as you can get and don't know how to get undisplaced."

Unutilized nurturers—like many older women—need a variety of help and services, from good role models to better housing and income benefits to job training and career planning to psychological counseling and help in making new friends. As these items indicate, re-engaging is a complex matter. It has both hazards and gratifications as the discussion in the next chapter will show.

CHAPTER 3

Re-engaged Nurturers

NURTURERS ARE women who see themselves primarily as givers to others, having absorbed this definition from parents, males, other women, the media, and society in general. We have seen what happens to such women when they lose the objects of their nurturance and, sometimes simultaneously, their economic base. Re-engaged nurturers are women who have lost husbands or families but found new people to nurture.

Some women have or adopt children late in life or become foster mothers. They may hold paid or volunteer nurturant jobs, remarry with the intent to nurture, and practice similar re-engagements. Sometimes their solutions are good ones; at other times, they are unfortunate. Thelma is one re-engaged nurturer who is happy in that role. After her six children grew up she became a Welcome Wagon hostess, gaining much satisfaction from settling newcomers into town. She particularly enjoyed helping them find services for their children. She has sometimes thought, however, that she should go back to school to prepare for work that would be better paid and more challenging.

When her oldest son graduated from college and her youngest entered, Bonita adopted a six-month-old girl of mixed race. Two years later she adopted a handicapped four-year-old brother for Tina. It amused Bonita that people thought she was the children's grandmother. She has tremendous patience with these children and has handled Tina's mixed racial identity and George's handicap with mature wisdom. She and her husband gave them warmth and life chances they would never have had otherwise. They worry a bit that Bonita will be in her sixties and her husband seventy when the children are late adolescents. But on the whole life is good.

After her children were grown up, Marian began to take the preschool children of working mothers into her home. She loves doing this, and the money is nice but not essential.

Patricia took longer to re-engage. She dreaded the day her last child left home and called her so frequently that her daughter finally said: "For Pete's sake, Mom, get somebody else to mother, I'm grown up." Patricia took the hint and volunteered at a school for exceptional children. Each year she has new children to help and she is happy. Phone calls to her daughter are now less frequent.

There are many women like Patricia. In fact, during my two years as an assistant dean of students at Boston University, I was surprised to learn that a large proportion of the young people who came for counseling complained that their mothers would not let them go. One told me he brought his mother a puppy to take his place. Others expressed guilt that their departure had caused so much distress. Some told me they invented (or perhaps created) minor problems to discuss so that their mothers would still feel needed. Their real problems they wanted to solve for themselves.

Nurturing on the Job

Inveterate nurturer Patricia became a re-engaged nurturer without really exploring what other options were open to her. Many "retired moms" rush into helping paid or volunteer jobs in teaching, nursing, social service, hospital, or library work. Some take seemingly non-nurturant clerical positions if they seem to offer nurturant possibilities. Such women become "Lady Fridays" who mother their bosses, get their coffee and lunch, handle their hostility, do a lot of their work, and cover up for them with patients, clients, or supervisors. They never feel put upon when overworked, underpaid, and unappreciated because, after all, they are HELPING.

The older saleswoman who asks "May I help you?" usually means it. She has a service orientation, but she is a vanishing breed. Many older women used to satisfy their helping habit by working in stores that gave personal service. The rapid growth of self-service business has eliminated this source of jobs for many older women. When one long-established Boston specialty store, R. H. Stearns, closed its shops a few years ago, the older women who had worked there for years were desolate. It was hard or impossible for them to find similar jobs; speedy young people are preferred to rack and ring up in self-service operations. Even if older women can get these jobs, they do not find them gratifying, for they provide no personal interaction or opportunity to help people directly.

With the rise of automation, computerization, and profit motives in other areas too, there are really few jobs that offer ex-nurturers the kind of expressivity or altruism they desire. Even though there are many unmet social needs in this country, there are too few paid positions for women who want to meet them. And most older women also need money; volunteering is declining as inflation increases.

It is like running a familiar tape to listen to the women at the workshops I run for alumnae who want to return to work. Usually it has been fifteen, twenty or more years since their graduation. Even though their clothes are three years out of style and they obviously need money to put the kids through college, almost all of them announce, "I want to work with people. I like to help others." Though they don't put it that way, they are really asking how can they continue to nurture. They seldom inquire which jobs pay the best or are the most plentiful or offer the most advancement. Yet these are indeed appropriate questions; at 40, a woman may work thirty years until retirement; at 50, twenty.

Often incorrectly, these women assume they have no capacities but nurturance. Actually homemakers often have great organizational, technical, and managerial ability.

Further, as we have already seen, many women perceive

themselves as failures because their children did not turn out precisely as they or their husbands had dreamed. They blame themselves rather than society and its institutions. By engaging in a second round of nurturance outside the family, they attempt to recoup what they perceive as their nurturant sins. In this, they are victims of their experience, indoctrination, and guilt propaganda. Social scientists, the media, therapists, clergy, and others have all, at one time or another, blamed mothers.

It is interesting that the same society that devalues older women attributes to them tremendous powers they do not possess. One outstanding male psychiatrist, Silvano Arieti, has pointed out that children are not simply blotters soaking up what mothers offer. The idea that the "pathological mother" is to blame for whatever happens in the family is, fortunately, being rethought, although there is always some cultural lag. Old myths and rumors persist long after they are "officially" debunked. Partly they persist because they serve the interests of those who spread and believe them. It takes the responsibility off men and society as a whole to blame vulnerable women for spoiling "their" children. This is clearly an easier and certainly cheaper solution than changing the schools, the media, the economy, and so on. This hypocrisy is similar to the government's policy of insisting on warnings on cigarette packages and blaming smokers but paying high subsidies to tobacco growers so government can reap the high taxes on tobacco and the votes of the farmers.

If the guilt of society is projected upon women, it can continue in its destructive ways while feeling it has done something—found a villain and pointed its finger. Naming and blaming a scapegoat, usually a victim, is common and stupid. Few social problems are the faults of individuals or aggregates of them. Social problems such as battered children or delinquent youth come from structural arrangements that do not provide human beings with security, happiness, or community.

Women Blamed Again

There are unexpected consequences in the current and needed interest in battered children. Certainly such children and the tragic parents who batter them should be helped. However, if the problem is spotlighted and the families actually get little real help, the public furor will simply add to the complaints against mothers and heighten their own self-blame. Mothers who batter their children are generally desperate women who wish they did not. Poor women who know they should not have more children are denied abortions by government policies and then condemned because, overburdened, exhausted, and frustrated, they turn against the unwanted children. Society blames them, but it does not help them.

Too often nurturers have also been blamed for crises in other areas. Mental illness is not caused exclusively by mothers, in spite of the cruel, irresponsible young male psychiatrist who told one older woman: "I will try to undo what you did to your poor son." The mother, a 50-year-old-woman named Phyllis withdrew into a deep depression that lasted for years. She had done her best after her husband nearly abdicated his responsibilities and let her raise three children with no help and very little money.

Such women, feeling they "should have done better," try to expiate by doing better, somewhere, the only thing they think they know—nurturing. Having lost their maternal identity or having been injured in it, they are now encountering new social norms that ascribe valued status only to those who achieve outside the home. "What do you do with yourself now that the children are grown?" people ask.

Is it any wonder that, pushed by guilt, peer pressure, finances, or boredom to seek jobs, they demand nurturing ones? After all, there are very few female role models to follow into other kinds of work. Women workers are still largely clustered in the clerical or helping professions.

Now there is nothing wrong with nurturing jobs – except that there are just not enough of them, they pay poorly, and many are exploitive and give no opportunity for advancement. As the old tale goes, some of my best friends nurture at work. Indeed, I chose to be a college professor because I could continue to be a Jewish mother, as well as a scholar, forever. However, getting academic jobs when I started teaching in the late sixties and getting tenure when I did in 1973 was a great deal easier than it is now.

There is a glut of professors, teachers, social workers, nurses, and almost all such professionals in almost all parts of the United States. Young women want these jobs too, and now men are taking some of them in the tough and cold world of nearly 6 percent unemployment. There are, of course, exceptions. There are still ads for physical and occupational therapists, due to the fact that, there are relatively few schools churning them out. Other departments continually dump their hapless nurturant professionals onto lengthy waiting lists. Very few schools advise entering students of the lack of jobs in their professions.

So, while re-engaging in paid nurturance seems a likely solution for many older women, not all can achieve it. Before investing in training for such occupations or pounding the pavements, women might do well to investigate other jobs for which they currently qualify or can learn to qualify. They might also consider that while little children are indeed appealing, and even adolescents occasionally have charm, there are other needy populations. Many employees of nursing homes hate their clients and work in them only because they cannot get other jobs. You can imagine what it is like to be chronically ill or old and be taken care of by people who don't like you. There is a shortage of sheltered workshops, daycare centers, and other services for the rapidly growing population of frail, elderly people. The number of persons over 75 will soon triple and are sources of paid and volunteer work for mid-life women. Unhappily, many mid-life and older women are so afraid of becoming frail themselves that they do not want to be around such people.

Louise, a widow of 60, is one such woman. Although she has insomnia and headaches, she has been told by her doctor that there is nothing physically wrong with her. He says she needs something to fill her hours. So Louise, who is indeed unhappy living alone, decided to be a Pink Lady volunteer at the local, suburban hospital. She thought it would be lovely to bring the bookmobile to people, wheel the new mothers and their babies out to the lobby, greet visitors at the reception desk, and take flowers to the rooms. She was crushed when the hospital thanked her politely saying they already had more volunteers than they could use, which was true. Louise has no automobile and is not close to public transportation so she cannot go to the city, where the hospitals might really need her. In any case in the city older women alone are prime mugger's targets.

I urged Louise to use her considerable energy, ability, and charm to volunteer at one or two nursing homes within walking distance of her home. Both are dreary places, and she could help a great deal by just talking to the lonely people and being a presence to prevent patient abuse. However, Louise refused: "I may be in one some day. I don't want to go to one now. No thanks." When I suggested that she could be a friendly visitor or paid homemaker for the homebound elderly, she refused, for a similar reason.

Of course, not all would-be re-engagers turn down the available opportunities. Indeed, much of the limited warmth that exists in institutions and bureaucracies comes from kind, under-recognized, and unrewarded mid-life women. Many older women have been able to get paid jobs using the nurturant skills developed in their families.

Education for Re-engagement

Maria is an example of this pattern. She had graduated as an art history major from an excellent college at age 21 and married that June. There were no jobs for art historians in the small rural town where her husband practiced dentistry; so she worked without wages as his receptionist and sterilized his instruments until her first child was born, eighteen months after marriage. By the time the children were all in school, the town and Bob's practice had both grown, and he had a full-time dental hygienist. At 35, Maria wanted a career of her own, one that would let her work part-time until the children were out of the house. It seemed impractical to stay in art history and she was now more interested in people than art. So she enrolled in the local community college, feeling uneasy about having Bob pay the tuition. (She forgot that she had worked free for eighteen months when he was starting his practice and that her homemaking had left him free to earn money.) She took a two-year program at the undergraduate level and received an associate of arts degree in para-professional social work; it qualified her to be a case aide. She had briefly considered a master's of social work program, since she already had a B.A. but she was afraid no school would admit her so many years after graduation. She also hated to ask Bob to spend the money for an expensive university; besides it was a long commute and she wouldn't have arrived home before the kids. Moreover, she felt unsure of herself.

After graduation, she got a case aide job at a family service agency, receiving half the salary of a M.S.W. Because of her maturity and ability, however, she was soon allowed to handle cases on her own and do about everything the M.S.W.'s did. She loved her work and was glad she had gone back to school, though sometimes she wished she had gone for the M.S.W.

Maria's experiences, compared to many older women's, add up to a success story. She was probably correct in believing that the master's program might not have admitted her. Women of all ages try frantically to get into M.S.W. programs. I spend a lot of time begging admissions people to accept my terrific young sociology graduates and older women — all of whom have done extensive volunteer work. Although some schools of social work have programs for older returnees, many are prejudiced against them. Their official stance is that they must invest their limited resources in women who have more years to give the profession. Besides, they contend, older women are too set in their ways. The real reasons may be quite different.

Here is what happened to Dorothy, a very bright, active, personable and well-motivated 39-year-old woman. She had just finished a B.A. summa cum laude, had excellent references from her professors, and had done a good deal of social service in her community when her three children were young. The prestigious graduate school of social work to which she applied called her in for an interview. The faculty member, a single woman who had been in the profession all her life, discouraged and discomforted Dorothy at the beginning of the interview by declaring: "We have a lot of trouble with older students."

Then she asked: "What would you do if you were on a case in your internship and your supervisor, who was younger than you, told you to handle a client you had been seeing for some time in an entirely different way than you had been doing?"

Dorothy replied: "Well, I would ask her why she thought we should change the treatment. If there were good reasons for changing and I was wrong, I would certainly want to follow her advice and improve."

The interviewer persisted. "Suppose she gave you an explanation you thought was nonsense."

Dorothy blanched, but answered honestly: "If she had never seen the client and I had been seeing the client for a long time, it would be difficult to follow advice that seemed injurious to the client's progress." By her frankness, Dorothy had flunked the test and was rejected. She was heartbroken and blamed herself, of course, for "lousing up my interview." A few years later, a more savvy candidate treated similarly, said "I'll see you in court," and the school relented.

Many entrenched, rigidified men and women of all ages, in the professions and in academia, feel threatened by mature returnees. My study of older women students supported by the Boston University graduate school turned up women at various universities and programs who had had very bad experiences with admissions officers, administrators, and faculty members. At one college, the part-time program for middle-aged women was eliminated because a young administrator thought that "older women take up too much of our time." Other women had marvelous relationships throughout their academic careers, although almost all experienced some stress.

With enrollments from traditional students declining many schools are now wooing returnees who can pay. Women who need financial aid, however, especially for part-time programs, have a much harder time. In addition, many classes are scheduled for hours inconvenient for older persons—who are freshest early in the day—and for women with homemaking responsibilities. It is traditional, for example, in many schools to schedule graduate courses 4:00 to 6:00 P.M. or at night.

This means that the woman who wants to prepare to re-engage while her adolescents are still at home must sacrifice having dinner with them and her husband, if she has one. In effect, to be ready for the next phase, the empty nest, she must be conflicted in the present stage. If she waits too long, until the children are in college, it may be more difficult to get into school or obtain employment. So if required classes are around the dinner hour, the usual time for family reunions, she has to make a hard choice.

It is understandable that universities offer many courses in the late afternoons or evenings to meet the needs of working people or graduate students who are teaching fellows during earlier hours. However, while many would-be re-engagers can take advantage of late-hour courses, others would be happier going to classes during the day, while their children and husbands are away. Although some colleges offer morning or early afternoon programs for returnees, programs leading to prestigious degrees in the nurturant professions are seldom so arranged. Neither their scheduling nor their requirement make allowances for nurturant types who put home responsibilities first while their children are still at home. Unlike careerists, whom we will discuss in another chapter, nurturers always put home first, and this puts them in conflict with most available college schedules.

Moreover, the older the would-be re-engager, the more difficult it is to have old credits accepted or get new ones. If I had not pushed at age 36 to start college, I would not have had my Ph.D. by 45 and tenure at 48. Ten years is about the minimum time in which to go from start to doctorate. Even a master's degree is a long haul, especially part-time, for a woman who starts without a B.A. Remember that many women now in their forties and fifties never went to college and that relatively few interesting and fairly well-paying nurturant jobs in the helping professions can be obtained with less than a master's. Right now I am advisor to a worried divorcée who will not get her doctorate until she is nearly fifty. In today's teaching market, she is going to need a lot of luck, for many employers prefer younger women—perhaps for the same reason they prefer younger sexual partners: decorativeness, naiveté, docility, speed, and so on. They often fail to recognize the value of the special devotion, judgment, and conscientiousness that are ingrained traits of many older women.

Nurturing Needs, But No Jobs

The infuriating thing is that America spends more on liquor and tobacco than on its social services. Poorer countries often have human services that are superior to ours. If we really staffed our educational and public services properly, there would be plenty of paid work for nurturant mid-life women. There is important work to be done for the poor, lonely, sick, and undereducated, but there are few positions. In Boston, School Volunteers, an organization, does match nurturers with need. What a shame that schools have to beg for volunteers to give children the attention they need! Many institutions cannot even use volunteers because they do not have the funds for a professional to train and supervise them.

CETA, the federal program to train the unemployed for jobs by using them in nonprofit agencies, until recently focused entirely on the young unemployed—certainly a needy group. The 1978 inclusion of displaced homemakers is a step forward, but perhaps we need to supplement the program with NETA, Nurturers Employment Training Act—for women who have employed husbands but want to work in human services.

Some desperate older women take any job they can get, nurturant or not. They usually make the best of it and enjoy the contacts with fellow employees and whatever gratifications they can get from it. But many are very badly exploited and work hard for low wages. So what else is new?

Even worse, many older women cannot get jobs at all. They lack job-seeking skills as well as job skills. They feel unsure, and the quick rejection they get confirms their unsureness. Older women with too much make-up and dressed in clothes too young can be seen at any employment agency begging for jobs they have no chance of getting. There is an almost universal prejudice against them. Despite federal legislation against age discrimination in employment, there is practically no money for enforcement.

Besides, nurturers, having been altruistic throughout their lives, rarely fight: they don't want to make trouble for anyone. A vicious self-fulfilling prophecy is established: because people treat them as inadequate, they feel inadequate and give up. To get a job, nurturing or otherwise, older women cannot be shy; but too many of them were taught to be a "good girl" and a "lady." In their view, assertiveness is simply bad manners.

If an older woman wants to nurture and has the qualifications for a position, she must be more persistent than anyone else. Seeking work against odds is analogous to the situation I faced in the blizzard of February 1978, which seemed to have dumped most of the heaviest snow of the century on my driveway. There was no way that a 53-year-old woman with a recently broken wrist could shovel, and none of my neighbors or their kids were available – they had enough trouble digging themselves out. After flagging down sixteen plows, I finally found a man willing to plow my driveway – for $50 cash in advance! Halfway through he stopped and asked for another $20. What else could I do to get to work?

Like me and the plowing, older women who want a chance to nurture usually have to struggle for it.

Re-engagement at Home

Some women re-engage primarily in the domestic sphere rather than in the work place. As we saw in the case of Laura (Chapter 1), many women with grown children spend considerable attention and energy on their husbands and relatives, including elderly ones. Others, who have lost spouses, like Deborah (Chapter 2) fantasize that they will find a new husband with whom they can resume an accustomed role. Although divorcées and widows frequently do re-engage in nurturance by remarrying, outcomes vary widely. Take Liza, for example;

Liza, a widow with two children, entered a second marriage and had two children in her late thirties. However, the second marriage failed and she found herself with two young children to rear alone; her two adolescents were too busy with their own lives and crises to give her much help. In the morning Liza takes care of an old person, and at night she works as a sales clerk. Afternoons, she tries to meet the needs of her six- and seven-year-olds. She is always exhausted and worried about money and about how long the older children will be willing to babysit while she works.

Other remarried women are happier. Annette is one. For twenty years she was married to a man who drank too much and gave her too little money and affection. She stayed with him because she hoped he would stop drinking someday and because "Junior and Polly need a father." However, when he broke her rib in a drunken rage, the children informed her that she could stay if she wanted but they were leaving. So she left with them and es-

tablished a new home for herself and the teenagers. She got a job
as a bookkeeper in a small business. When Junior went into the
navy and Polly took a secretarial job in Washington, Annette
agreed to marry Dan, her employer, whose wife had died the year
before. He had two grown children and a boy in his last year of
high school.

Junior and Polly like Dan. Annette and Dan's youngest son
get along as well as adults and adolescents generally do. Dan and
Annette are so happy together that their friends say they are like
young lovers. She loves keeping house for him and tells her
friends she feels like a bride; she keeps buying cookbooks and
trying new recipes to surprise him. Although she hadn't sewn for
years, she made new draperies. Cases like this true story, which
sounds like a soap opera, do happen.

In fact, even women who have never been married before
sometimes re-engage in nurturing late in life. Cecilia, at 38, was
a nursing supervisor when she met and married a 55-year-old
hospital administrator and became stepmother to his three adolescent children. Lynette, a secretary of 35 who had long wanted
to be married, wed a 50-year-old executive and took on his four
half-grown children. Some of the older women in the office were
angry because such a "good catch" had selected a woman 15 years
his junior rather than a woman nearer his own age.

Large numbers of older widows and divorcées also remarry.
Barbara Vinick and I wrote (in our book, *Re-engagement in Later
Life*) about women over the age of 65 who found new spouses.
When asked why they remarried at ages ranging from 65 into the
80s, these women generally said they wanted "someone to take
care of." In fact, one lady in a wheelchair remarked that she married her husband so she could help him; and indeed she joyfully
did some small chores for him.

Jean Baker Miller has written that the giving qualities of
half the human race, women, should be considered before we con-
clude that humans are innately aggressive. Whether women are
innately more altruistic than men or become givers through

socialization is certainly debatable. Nonetheless, in our society women often do not feel justified unless they are able to live for someone else.

This characteristic of women is reflected in the fact that many older women who live alone don't cook much for themselves, even though they once cooked well for families or spouses. This is not simple laziness. These women somehow consider it self-indulgent to labor just for themselves. Alone they will eat from paper plates and consume junk food they would never serve anyone else; but for a guest they will prepare a great meal and use their best dishes. One woman, Eleanor, states: "I always keep something nice in the freezer ready to cook if my son shows up." But when she is alone, Eleanor usually has cereal or yogurt for dinner.

Meeting and Not Meeting Men

Many women in their late thirties, forties, fifties, and sixties would love to meet men, but they do not know how or where. Married young, some of them do not know how to go about seeking a mate late in life. Women are now living longer, and marriages are breaking up more often. Yet, there are few arrangements to deal with the problem. In the age of tradition the marriage broker sought to have no available widow unmatched; he was a trusted ally. Nowadays the matchmakers are computer dating services and newspaper personal columns.

Many older women would rather be alone than take chances on such arrangements. They are scared by the murders, rapes, and other crimes featured in the media and uneasy about the propriety of such services. Other women feel differently (see Chapter 9), but probably the majority of older women would not go to a singles' bar, club, or weekend. Their reluctance is reinforced by the stories they hear from those who do venture out.

Lilly, 45, after retreating to the safety of a widows' club, described her experiences at a singles' dance she attended with another woman. Their hopes of dancing and perhaps meeting "some nice men" were dashed when two men came over and said: "let's not bother to dance; let's go right to our apartment and cuddle."

Marian, a vivacious and witty woman of about fifty then recounted her story. "My husband died a year ago. We had a very good life together, and my life pretty much revolved around him after the kids were grown. When he died, I missed him terribly and could not bear the thought of living the rest of my life without a husband. I felt incomplete, like a half person. I began to go to events where I thought there might be single men. I also took some vacations at places where I might meet men. I know this sounds cold blooded, but I felt desperate. I did meet men, but all of them wanted to go to bed as soon as we met, and I felt degraded. I believe sexual intimacy should be within marriage, and I am certainly not promiscuous. I met one man I liked very much, but he told me he was not interested in marriage. If I would not let him share my bed he would not see me; there were plenty of women who would," Lilly butted in: "Values have changed." Marian replied: "I know, but I haven't."

Marian has not given up on her effort to re-engage, however, she concluded her comments by asking the other women whether they knew any place in the U.S., or even abroad, "Where I could find a nice man who would be interested in marriage?"

Marian is a determined woman. She feels unable to exist as a single individual after so many years of mutuality. Other widows, just as bereft, do not seek other men; they feel that to do so would be somehow traitorous.

Indeed many even feel guilty because they have outlived their mates. Over and over again, they ask themselves how they might have cared for him better and prevented his death. The emphasis on the relation of diet to heart trouble has added to the guilt of these already guilt-prone women. They learned to cook in an era when butter and cream were considered good ingredients, not possible elevators of cholesterol. Many women married in the

1940s or 1950s used the *Fanny Farmer Cookbook*, which should perhaps be titled "Fatty Farmer" because of the high fat content of many of its recipes. These women now agonize over every steak and cream pie they served their husbands and wonder if their men would have lived longer if they had taken it easier. Mary bewails the fact that "he always shoveled the snow and carried the heavy bundles, and worked for and opened doors for little me. Now he's dead at sixty, and little me is alive and well, feeling bad at what he did, though he wanted to."

Nurturing Other Women

Although some agonize about the quality of their past nurturance, most confirmed nurturers re-engage in some way or search for ways to do so. In the absence of available men, some women turn to nurturing other women, sexually and emotionally. Even those who reject lesbianism sometimes direct their nurturant energies toward other women, cooking and doing errands for them. When this is a mutual arrangement of women caring for each other, it may help. However, what frequently happens is that women with a need to nurture meet needy ones who are glad to have them do so. Under these circumstances the same kind of exploitation often characteristic of male-female relations can ensue. The nurturer who does not receive reciprocal nurturance may go on indefinitely in the martyr role, or she may rebel. One forty-year-old woman held perpetual open house for her friends at her summer cottage feeding and entertaining them. She finally rebelled when a visiting friend brought in and handed her a full ashtray from her car, expecting her to empty it! The hostess hated the smell of old tobacco in her house. Until then, though she had secretly resented serving as perpetual hostess, she had put up with it.

More often, I think, the warm support older women give each other makes life tolerable. Indeed, older women provide wonderful and rare models of thoughtfulness and giving. Who else but an older woman, my friend Grace Vicary, would have thought to plant strawberries in large planters as soon as she knew I bought a house so that when I moved in she could bring me strawberry plants to enrich my patio and my table all summer?

In all, there are many kinds of re-engagers or would-be re-engagers, and their paths lead in many directions. What they have in common is the central theme of their lives—the desire to get gratification from giving loving help, service or interest to others. Not everyone, of course, shares their preoccupation—not even all the older women, as we shall see in the next chapters.

CHAPTER FOUR

Chum Networkers and Leisurists

IT MAY SEEM odd to group together networks of ethnic wives, church women, tennis players, socialites, suburbanites, leisurists, divorcees, widows, lesbians, hedonists, older welfare and project mothers, working women, and hobbyists. What these women share is a salient identity that comes from passing time with like-minded women in an attempt to extract some pleasure from life, dispel boredom, or offer mutual support and affection. The important things to them are fun and friendship. Community centers, health clubs, craft courses, tennis courts, theaters, restaurants, resorts, and many other places are full of such older women.

Even when there are men or paid or volunteer work in their lives, women of this type spend a great deal of time seeking pleasure, alone or with female chums. They may be suburban or ethnic wives whose husbands spend little time with them because of the demands of their occupation or subculture. They may be members of widow and divorcée cliques. They may be women, poor or middle class, who live together in housing projects or neighborhoods and provide each other with a sense of community or at least companionship. They may be never-married women who work full time because they need money but who consider the recreational time spent with women friends the vital and interesting part of their lives.

Some chum networkers and leisurists are mothers whose children are grown. Because of their visibility, the number of depressed older women, mothers of "empty nests," may be overestimated, for apron strings tie both ways. Though not without some guilt and anxiety, many women report experiencing a kind of renaissance during widowhood or after divorce or when grown children leave home. They thrive on hobbies, friendships, and self-development. One summed it up by saying: "For the first time in many years I can really enjoy life and do things for myself." Motherhood is full of ambivalences that must be constantly repressed, and many women experience enormous relief when their mothering is done.

Such women who are employed like their jobs but enjoy leisure activities more; others hate their work or endure it as an economic necessity. Vacation travel and recreation are tremendously important to them; and they anticipate vacations with pleasure and savor them for long months afterward. Most older women are underemployed at demeaning jobs or they are unemployed. For gratification outside of working hours or to fill time without jobs such women rely on individual recreations or passing time with women in the same boat.

Many women of the older generations are married to men who hold the traditional view that males should earn the living, while females do housework and keep busy with expressive functions. Wives should spend time on the home and with relatives—including the sick or aging of both sides of the family—visit grandchildren, and organize the couple's social and recreational activities. Many husbands believe that wives are entitled to hobbies or recreation with "girlfriends" during the day as long as dinner is on the table when they come home. Among some groups it is a sign of "success" to support a well-dressed wife in leisure. These same men feel they would lose their "hold" over a wife who was financially independent. Other older men are unsure of themselves, threatened by change, or fear that a working wife will be seduced by the world or other men.

Affluent couples frequently have homes that require considerable care; they may entertain and garden lavishly, requiring much work from the wife. Ironically, at an age when many older women are tired of family-centeredness, older men are likely to become enamoured of the comforts of hearth and home. They love it when the children leave and the wife is theirs exclusively.

Other men resent the fact that they must struggle daily in an uncongenial job while their wives seem to be having a fine, free time. Especially if the erotic interest has cooled or gone elsewhere, such a wife may find herself nagged, put on a skimpy allowance, or prompted—by her husband or her own discontent—to do paid work. At this point she may develop into a careerist, the type to be discussed in the next chapter. More often she will end up with the typical inferior, no-growth older women's job. In that case, if her relationship with her husband has deteriorated, she may come to derive her chief gratification from hobbies or her women friends. Occasionally she is so exhausted by the demands of home, uncongenial work, and a difficult husband that she becomes ill (see Chapter 8). Generally, however, the women described in this chapter center their lives around recreations and relationships. Several examples are given in this chapter. The first is Sharon and Elaine:

Sharon, at 50, has a trim body that shows up well in her tennis outfit. She and Tim, her physician husband, live in a large, rather empty house, for the four children are married or off pursuing careers. Sharon married Tim after her junior year at a midwestern college and accompanied him to New York for his internship. There she finished college just a month before the birth of her first child. Sharon has worked as a hospital volunteer but held a paid job for only three years, while the youngest three children were in college simultaneously. Then, even a doctor's income was strained, and Sharon "helped out." But the job was a dead end, and she didn't mind leaving it when Tim objected that she was always exhausted and the house was a mess. Now Sharon shops with friends, has coffee in the morning or lunch "with the girls," and joins them in a drink or two in the afternoon after tennis. Recently she took a ceramics course and makes wedding gifts for friends' and relatives' children.

Sharon's best friend is Elaine, whose husband has to travel on business a great deal. When he is away, Sharon is delighted because Elaine can play tennis, go to museums, and visit other places with her when Tim is at the hospital on weekends. In fact, because Sharon's husband almost never leaves his patients and Elaine's husband is sick of traveling, the two women often take trips together. They actually spend more of their waking hours together than with their mates. Although both women are happy in their marriages, they find it easier to talk to each other than to their husbands.

Sharon is terrified that some day Elaine may have to move if her husband is relocated; and Elaine would hate it too because she has become so dependent on Sharon. Both are vaguely discontented at times, and feel slightly guilty about it. After all, they have nice homes and husbands and enjoy each other and other friends. Still, on the whole they enjoy life—or say they do.

Simply enjoying the good life is sometimes not quite enough for women like Sharon and Elaine. They feel that they have not justified their existences since the children grew up. During our interview, Sharon told us three times that she makes wedding presents and collects clothes for the hospital thrift shop. Especially if they are well educated and aware of human misery, such women are nagged by conscience as they play out their consumeristic roles. Sometimes they use strange ways to prove their value. Their need for validation is illustrated by the following conversation recorded in the locker room of an exclusive golf club. Two leisurists are sitting over gin and tonics on a weekday afternoon.

Woman 1 (about 50): Susanna is doing her house over again. She has hired an interior decorator.

Woman 2 (a little younger): *I have no respect for anyone who has to hire a decorator. When I do my house over, I can make my own choices. I have good taste.*

Woman 1: *Me too. Susanna is nouveau riche. She has no class.*

Woman 2: *Yes, her house is gaudy. It is a pleasure to walk into your house.*

Woman 1: *And yours.*

Denise still gets Aid to Families with Dependent Children (AFDC) because her two youngest children are in high school. She hopes they will finish, although many of the adolescents in her housing project drop out. Her husband was a dropout and could never get a good job. Discouraged, he finally drifted away from the family, and she does not know his whereabouts.

Denise feels that her three older children really learned very little in school to train them for jobs. She had ambitions for them and was sad when the two boys went into the Army and Lisa took a job as a hotel maid.

Denise herself works as a cleaning lady when she can get day work. Then, she rides on a bus filled with other black women traveling from the dirty, crowded city to the totally white suburbs. At each stop, several of the women are dropped off and picked up by their "white ladies," who return them to the bus late in the afternoon. The husbands of the employers ride the bus in the reverse direction–into the city by day and out to the greenery at night. Denise is fearful that even this unpleasant day work is drying up because many suburbanites are turning to mechanized cleaning services–usually males driving out in automobiles. Without transportation or training, Denise does not know what other kind of work she can get. Soon the last child will be 18, and her AFDC will stop. The social worker has urged her to get a full-time job, but nobody seems to want to hire a black woman of fifty with only day work references.

Denise gets little joy from her work and not much money; she can hardly wait to leave the lovely suburb to get home to the project, ugly as it is. In good weather, she likes to sit on the bench in the courtyard and talk to her women friends. When they have money, they attend movies together or sit in "their restaurant" over a cup of coffee or a beer. Whoever has money treats. They often discuss moving out of the project and near better schools, but they don't know how to do it. One woman in the project is going to college on scholarship, and she has become "uppity" and won't sit down and talk to them, saying she has to write papers. She makes them uncomfortable and, though they help each other, they figure "if she is so smart, she can do for herself." Most of the women of this mutual-support clique have lost their men in one way or another, often to younger women. Denise does not think life is too bad however; after all, she has good friends who would do anything for her, as she would for them. They even laugh together a lot—what else can they do? It is very hard to get off that bench, especially when there is little knowledge of how to do so; it means giving up friends for a lonely, unfamiliar, and rejecting world.

The new provision for retraining displaced housewives under CETA could help some Denises if a real effort is made to reach these women and to give them training that will lead to permanent jobs. Often in the past poor minority persons have received training for jobs that never materialized—either because of unrealistic training, economic conditions, or continuing prejudice among employers. The displaced housewives program may also be effected by a drastic cut in CETA funding made in late 1978.

As both private and public colleges experience severe financial pressures, even fewer opportunities will be available for poor older students. Without financial aid, emotional support, and good counseling, it is hard or impossible for people whose original education was poor to plug into regular programs. The resources to provide the special transitional help they need are in very short supply, and it is a rare older, minority, poor woman who has the opportunity of Denise's neighbor. It is much easier for middle and upper class women—with their good early education and knowledge of how to tap resources—to be retrained late in life. Denise is a bright woman, and her children had potential. But because of poor schools none of them received the background, encouragement, or finances needed for further education. The chances are they will have lifetimes of frustration; Denise's daughters may end up on a project bench as older women.

Because of segregated living, there are usually no role models for the poor or peer support for mobility. In many ethnic or working-class communities the person who seeks to go beyond the status of the group must have a great capacity to withstand social stress. In blue-collar neighborhoods it is very difficult for an older woman to move beyond the traditional female roles. Her difficulties are compounded by the rejection she often experiences as she tries to become an academic or professional. The older woman who is also divorced or widowed may need the services of her neighbors to care for her children; but she is in danger of losing their help if she violates community norms.

Even in the middle and upper classes, it is very hard for an older woman to strike out where the group cannot or does not want to follow. To make new friends late in life is difficult; it is no wonder that many older women cling to those they have. Anne, a woman, more ambitious than her neighbors, tells the following story:

I lived for twenty-five years in the same stable neighborhood; my kids had played with the same friends since infancy. When I got my B.A. at age 40, the woman across the street honored me at a large luncheon to which she invited all the women on the street. She later got a B.A. herself, so I was a role model for her in a way. When I got my M.A., few of the women on the street congratulated me, although I saw them all at one time or another. When I got my Ph.D., the university sent out a release and my picture was in the local paper with the story, so everyone knew about it. None of the women on the street mentioned it except one close friend. I had gone beyond the status of the group, and everyone was uncomfortable. Although I still considered the neighbors my friends, they found my new job and life inconsistent with theirs, and I found myself having to make new friends. But this wasn't easy at my age.

The competent and successful woman also may be avoided by

men who feel threatened by her. Women recognize this possibility and, as Matina Horner's research indicated, fear success. When men avoid them, bright women are even more terrified of antagonizing their female friends; same sex friends can provide essential support for older women, who are a high risk group for emotional injury. They can cushion and comfort and compensate for unhappy realities. Passing time with them, however, can also prevent some women from moving into roles that, in the long run and with transitional pain, may bring better life chances. Every older women must decide for herself. Often, however, people do not make conscious choices; they just drift along with the familiar current. Very few alternate ways of life are presented to older women who are supported–and sometimes also disabled–by their networks. Yet they cannot be expected to give up their friends when other options are seen as, and often are, unattainable. Older women can find understanding among their kind, and, in an uncaring world, they surely need friendship. Mobility and stress are twins that present a dilemma to chum networkers; as long as they don't try to move they are unhappy with their lives but are supported by friends in the same situation.

For example, Madeline, now 40, was once married to a man who abused her physically and emotionally. She left him ten years ago when the children were 5 and 7 years old. They visit him twice a year for a week, and he sends a little money for them. He is remarried to a woman ten years his junior. Madeline has had several men in her life since the divorce, but the relationships did not lead to marriage. Either the men did not want to wed a woman with children or there were other impediments, including her own caution. Madeline has always held a job and manages to support the household at a modest level. She hopes their father will pay for the children's college or that they will get scholarships. Most of the women at Madeline's office are younger than she is. The few her age are married and occupied with their husbands on weekends, when her adolescents are also busy with their friends. Lately no men have appeared for Madeline, and she sees her nest emptying and loneliness as inevitable. She also "misses a warm body in bed."

Recently she saw an announcement in a woman's newspaper for a potluck supper. She went and found the women in the group friendly; many of them were in situations similar to hers. She enjoyed the Saturday potluck suppers and began to go other places with her new friends. It was wonderful to have something to do on the weekends. Shortly, however, she discovered, to her great shock, that the women were lesbians. She had always considered herself firmly heterosexual; she liked men, although the experience of her husband's cruelty made her somewhat distrustful of them. She had tried to be open minded about homosexuality, but underneath she felt it was not quite proper.

Although her new friends did not put direct pressure on her to live a gay life, they did talk a great deal about how exploitative men were, a fact Madeline knew well from her own relationship with lovers and bosses. They also spoke enthusiastically of the superior joys of women loving women. She had been looking for a long time for companionship, and it was hard to give up her friends. Soon she drifted into an affair with Beverly. When it broke up after only a few months, she began a more intense relationship with Francine, which she hoped would be permanent. Although she still didn't feel completely at ease in her new role, she had found both friends and a lover.

The readers may feel that Madeline should have been included in the chapter on re-engaged nurturers since she had re-established an intimate personal relationship. However, I wonder if many of the Madelines are turning to other women less out of sexual or nurturance needs, than out of a yearning for friendship and company. For some older women a long-term gay relationship is far more satisfying than filling their lives with "one-night stands" or affairs with married men.

Women like Madeline, who become single late in life, may find it difficult to meet compatible, single heterosexual women their own age. We have already mentioned the sad fact that many divorced women suddenly find their married friends unavailable or rejecting, whereas gay women may offer friendship and understanding, both rare commodities. Of course, many older women, unlike Madeline, refuse to consider lesbianism as healthy or moral. They may even become leery of *any* close relationship with women. They are thus doubly deprived—of both men and women.

To emancipate themselves from the subservient female role, some women feel they must choose other women as love objects; men, they say, offer them no path but inequality. Moreover, a woman hurt by men, as very many older ones have been, may express her anger indirectly by showing that she does not need them. As one said when her husband of 25 years began a series of affairs: "I'm going to learn to be a lesbian." Undoubtedly such a conscious determination is very rare. Although almost every human being has the potential for attraction to people of both sexes, a change of sexual preference is more a complex matter of gradual resocialization, personal need, inclination, and circumstances.

It is a sad fact that many people are always ready to give older women a bad name. Others, including some poor frightened nurturers, are eager to hurt the women's movement. People who are really against equality for women out of various motives have made altogether too much of the participation of lesbians in the women's movement and ERA ratification drive. It has got so bad that heterosexual women who used to kiss each other hello hesitate to use their usual greeting for fear of being tagged gay. More than one heterosexual academic has had gossip and tenure trouble because she can't produce a man in her life.

Only a small proportion of older women choose lesbianism. Those who do are drawn into the network of lesbians because it is vocal and because lesbian women have made an effort to set up supportive structures. Although there are some organizations for heterosexual older single women, the majority of them are composed of never-married or of young women, with whom older widows or divorcées may not have much in common. Many traditional community integrators, such as churches, have failed these women. Older women who have always been single have usually made their friends and their adjustments, and many have very full happy lives. But the woman whose time has been taken up with mothering may experience a tremendous gap in her life when she is suddenly alone; men pass her by and other women already have their routines. Widows in their fifties and beyond—and there are a great many of them—may suffer isolation and loneliness. Others, like Helena, find the chum network a solution to their situation.

Helena and her husband had a good life together and she mourned him deeply when he died at age 56; she was 52. She was glad that her job kept her busy. Selling towels is a boring business, however, and Helena was fortunate to have as chums three other widowed women. Mary, 60, was the liveliest and always knew where to go. The quartet had fun, going to dances (they rarely gave the men their phone numbers) and sitting at a rear table in "their" bar where they could watch and talk about what was happening. They did not envy the young mothers who were out with their husbands; they were glad they didn't have to be responsible for anyone and could stay as long as they liked.

Helena liked her little apartment, which was easy to keep clean. Mary and Genevieve, who didn't work, were urging Helena and Fran to take one morning off to join the local woman's bowling league. About twice a month, one of the four had the other three friends over for a nice meal. When it was her turn, Helena always cooked extra food so she would have plenty of leftovers. Usually she cooked very simply for herself. Even if her grown-up children forgot her birthday, it was nice to know that her friends would remember.

Certain older women fill time with social activities connected with their religious denominations. This has long been a source of interaction and integration for the older married woman and spinsters, especially in small towns and rural areas. However, the newly alone older woman may find it very traumatic to discover that she is devalued by the congregation, which is largely focused on the needs of the intact families. Some denominations still exclude or stigmatize divorcées; even those that do not seldom make provision for them or for widows after the funeral period.

Consider Thelma, who at age 53 was divorced and moved to a new community and a new job to get away from painful memories. She was very lonely and went to the church of her denomination the first Sunday after moving. Apparently she was noticed because one couple spoke to her after the service and invited her to the coffee hour in the parish house. Thelma's hopes rose. However, once inside, neither the couple nor anyone else spoke to her, though she is a quite pleasant, ordinary-looking woman. Everyone nearby was chattering, and she felt very left out and decided to leave. On the way out she signed her name and address in the guest book, and looked at the list of church organizations. There was a couples' club, a young people's group, a senior citizens' group, and a ladies auxiliary, which met during her working hours. "I don't belong anywhere," she thought and rushed out before anyone could see the tears in her eyes. Months later she heard from the church – an announcement of the annual giving campaign and a return envelope for her contribution.

Thelma, a would-be networker who found no help at the church of her denomination, had a very illustrative experience at another. Desperate to make friends, she went to a different church because she saw an announcement that there was a Saturday-night dinner and program for "singles over 35." She discovered that a marvelous nurturant single woman cooked a delicious meal every week and that attendees paid only the cost of ingredients. However, when she joined the diners, Thelma found some of them very strange. One young man, who was much younger than 35, had a toy fire engine with him, wore a fireman's hat, and kept making strange noises. A young woman, also well under 35, had a vacant look and would not respond to Thelma's "hello." It seems that a local mental health center had decided to send its patients to the Saturday night singles' group.

Thelma, whose self-esteem had already been injured by the divorce, found this almost too much to bear. She had a great deal of sympathy for the patients but resented that an older singles' activity should be considered the natural habitat of the maladjusted of all ages. She ventured out to no more groups. When someone at her workplace suggested she try a singles' bar, she pointed out she had never gone to bars in her life and doubted that she would meet people of her kind there.

The people of Thelma's first church were kind to old people, children, even pet stray animals. But somehow single, mid-life women were invisible to them which is surprising as there are now so many of them. The widow-to-widow program which has been very helpful to new widows, suggests the need for a similar "divorced-to-divorced" group. More media help for the Thelmas is also clearly needed. In Newton, Massachusetts, the Women's Co-op does run a once-a-week separation and divorce workshop, and Lucia Bequaert's book, *Single Women: Alone and Together,* does list resources. But more programs are needed, especially for older women divorcées.

Although there is certainly less stigma to divorce now, the woman who divorces late in life is sometimes still held suspect by herself and society. Nagged, in many cases, by an inner sense of failure, she may indulge in orgies of guilt. She is usually too much of a lady to tell friends or acquaintances of the abuse that drove her to divorce, or she is ashamed to speak ill of her children's father.

Unlike a widow, who can celebrate the virtues of him whom she has lost, the divorcée who has been rejected by a man cannot say much about him without being considered a poor loser or a complainer. She is expected to be a good sport and keep her resentment or grief bottled up, while the widow is encouraged to express hers.

Moreover, if she is fairly attractive, the divorcée is held in more suspicion than the widow, though widows too are feared by married women, according to their reports. The divorcée is considered fair game by men and a threat by married women, who do not want to be reminded that marriage can fail. Moreover, women who are divorced after their children are married often face hostility from children who are also defending themselves against the idea that it can happen to them.

An uneasy relationship with adult children makes it all the more important to have chums. But it is harder for divorcées to find friends than it is for widows, who are generally older and more likely to remain in the same community. Naomi, a newly divorced older woman and founding mother of her suburban temple, tells how she tried to join another when she moved, post-divorce, to a different suburb:

I was turned off because I discovered that every Friday night service, for the entire summer during the rabbi's vacation, was led by a married couple. I asked if there were any widowed, divorced, or never-married people in the congregation. The membership chairman said, "I think so, but we don't seem to attract a lot of these people or hold them." I said, "No wonder. You treat them like pariahs. Why didn't you pick one to lead a service to show they were part of things?" He became offended and said, "Why don't you join a congregation in the city where there are more singles?" I was very hurt. I'm not trying to be fixed up—I was just trying to educate him. I wanted to join a congregation in my town, but I guess singles don't belong there.

A never-married older woman tried to join a tennis and swim club in her community. She found that the membership fee for a single person was exactly the same as that for a family, even one with six children. Like most single women, her income was not good (women earn 40 percent less than men on the average). She felt that the price was unfair in view of the usage of the facilities and was convinced it was a deliberate attempt to exclude single people.

Single older women need the encouragement of friends, wherever they find them, for society offers them precious little support and help and often treats them like some strange, even ill, minority. Obviously there are many more kinds of chum networkers than have been described in our five cases. But, sadly enough, potential chum networkers cannot connect with each other.

Students who work as volunteers on crisis hot lines usually intended for young people report that many lonely older women call just to hear a human voice. Many also call into talk shows; some of these people talk too long, and it is clear they have no one else to talk to. The stereotype of the older spinster or widow who grabs a neighbor in the hall and won't let him or her escape probably has some truth to it. It is so difficult sometimes for such people to find human contact; even in stores or restaurants, they often have to wait until everyone else is served. Everyone avoids them. Some are easy prey to salesmen, who at least seem interested in them. Perhaps the bumper sticker Have you hugged your kid today, should be supplemented by one that reads Have you said hello to an older woman today? Some older women report it has been years since anyone touched them, weeks since anyone talked to them.

In any case, older women who do find peers to pass time with should not be ridiculed, as they so often are, as a "bunch of old hens." Humans need others. We do not consider adolescents who hang around together as a joke—though we may be annoyed by their noise. We consider it manly and appropriate if a bunch of men do something together. Why do we make jokes when women over 40 band together against a cruel world? Most of them are not lesbians, despite the snide remarks, and those who are have that right and also often no alternative.

If suburban wives drink too much in the afternoon with "the girls" and consume other things too conspicuously, it is because that is the role allotted them by their husbands and society. If women end up becoming isolates, escapists, or activists perhaps it is because, like Thelma, they could not find acceptance in traditional settings. If they sit on benches, like Denise, it is because nobody offers another seat.

But when networks are unavailable, pall, or disintegrate, or finances or ambitions compel, women often turn to paid work for life satisfaction. This is the subject of the next chapter.

CHAPTER FIVE

Careerists —Employed and Unemployed

CAREERISTS, though they may have husbands, children, friends or hobbies, derive their main identity and life satisfaction from paid work. Some have worked all their adult lives. Janice, who is now 40, has been single all her life.

"I didn't decide or set out to be single . . . nobody ever came along, and it just happened that way," she explains. She has held a middle-management position in a large corporation for some years and finds it very involving. There is so much work to do that she takes it home on weekends and often is at the office far into the evening. She has to visit regional offices three or four times a year. She enjoys these trips because she is very good at straightening out problems.

Janice is proud that she held a responsible job before the women's movement and knows that promotions follow devoted work. She started as a secretary, even though she had a B.A. in economics from an excellent college. She believes that if she were a man she would now be in a higher position, but she is reasonably content. She has few interests apart from her job. She earns a good salary, a considerable part of which she spends on clothes because, as she says, "I represent a very fine company." She takes short trips in the summer, often alone, but never minds returning because there is so much work waiting that "only I can do." Actually the "vacations" she likes best are taking management courses or going to conferences. They help her work, and she enjoys talking to people in other companies.

It is clear that Janice gets her human interaction and much

of her gratification through work. One might also say she is sublimating her personal needs through the corporation. At any rate, Janice, like many successful single women, is, despite myths to the contrary, among the healthiest most contented women in our society. She is good at her job, knows it, has excellent medical care, eats well (often in good restaurants), and enjoys numerous company benefits. She buys many gifts for nieces and nephews, and spends holidays with her sister's or brother's family. She used to envy her married sister; but now that her sister's marriage is disintegrating, Janice is not sure she has missed anything.

One of Janice's fringe benefits at the corporation is an excellent retirement plan, which is operational at 65; few people stay longer. The only thing that really bothers Janice is that her job will not last forever. She knows that some people have been bribed or pressured into leaving earlier, but she tries not to think about it—it scares her. She knows that a woman executive who retired two years ago at 60 seems happy living in a retirement community. She also knows that another recently left earlier than she wished to and is miserable.

Like Janice, older women in demanding jobs are often worried that they will not be able to keep up the pace, or that they will be considered obsolete, be dumped, and have empty lives. One of the problems for careerists of both sexes is that in order to advance they must sacrifice everything to their work; then, later in life, they find themselves without other interests. The prospect of retirement haunts many women, as it does men. Contrary to earlier research, it has now been found that women whose work was important have just as hard or harder retirement adjustments than men. For example, Philip Jaslow reported in the *Journal of Gerontology* that women who worked past 65 were better off psychologically than members of the retired control group. But adjusting to retirement at 65 or 70 is something many women careerists or would-be careerists never experience. Long before that age, they find themselves unemployed for a variety of reasons. Some retire early in order to join an older spouse who is retiring. This early retirement becomes a tragedy when the husband dies before the wife, leaving her without companionship, job, and, often, any opportunity for re-employment.

Women's Unemployment

While many older women continue their careers throughout life—or, after childrearing, re-enter or begin them successfully—more could do so were it not for prejudice, lack of adequate and inexpensive training, transportation problems, job shortages, and so on. (In 1976 only 9 percent of the trainees in the three major CETA title programs were over the age of 45.)

In my research on re-employment in old age, I found a number of women over 65 who were still quite productive at work; but I also found others who were forced to leave their jobs at about 50 and could not find others despite good skills. Rejection was so painful that many women simply gave up looking. Careerists at heart, they are unemployed in fact. Much of the considerable unemployment in this country is hidden because older people, after exhausting benefits, get discouraged and stop looking for jobs. Unemployment statistics reflect the numbers actively seeking work—not those electing not to work or those who have given up looking.

This situation is noted in a 1975 publication of the Bureau of Labor Statistics *Women in the Labor Force* (p. 15):

> It should be noted that many women, particularly those whose husbands work, may opt to drop out of the labor force if their job search appears fruitless, a factor which partially explains their shorter duration of unemployment.
>
> For both men and women, the duration of unemployment tends to increase with age. Nearly 25 percent of the women 45 to 54 years of age were unemployed 15 weeks or more, compared with 15 percent of women 25 to 34 years. Within the larger age group, single women had the longest spells of unemployment. Married women had an average (mean) duration of 8.3 weeks, compared with 12.5

weeks for single women, and 10.1 weeks for widowed, divorced, or
separated women. . . .

While a larger proportion of the younger women become unemployed, their duration of unemployment is shorter. Among women
who worked but were also unemployed at some time in 1974, 63
percent of those 25 to 34 years of age had 10 weeks or less of job-
lessness, compared with 58 percent of the women 35 to 54 years.

Thus, many older careerists, despite heroic efforts, are not
able to find jobs for which they are qualified. Often they are willing to take jobs below their ability and standard salaries, but
usually they are denied these jobs too, because they are "overqualified." Overqualified means that employers feel threatened
by them and would rather hire someone younger and less able but
more subservient. Re-enterers often suffer this kind of discrimination.

Cathryn is such a woman. While her four children were growing up, she attended school and got a laboratory technician's certificate at the age of 45. She was able to obtain some part-time
and temporary jobs at low salary and took them in order to gain
experience. However, she had no success in getting a full-time job,
and she began to feel very guilty about the money spent on her
schooling in the expectation that her earnings would later help
put the children through college. Her husband sympathized with
her situation and was encouraging through her job-hunting
traumas, but she became increasingly hurt and depressed. What
was most unfortunate was that she began to doubt her own competence. After repeated rejections she gave up the search for a
full-time job and settled for temporary work when she could get it.

Similarly discouraging experiences are reported by women
who have been in the labor market a long time—perhaps on a
part-time basis while their children were small—and by others
who withdrew temporarily to raise children. The older they are,
the harder it is to get a secure job. Government cuts and RIFS
(Reductions in force) by industry have hit older women returnees
especially hard. The last to come, they are the first fired. As hard

as they try to look younger, they often can find only exploitative part-time or short-term jobs—not employment that will last through a working lifetime extended by better health and a later retirement age.

In fact the extension of mandatory retirement to age 70 is adversely affecting the employment prospects of some older women returnees to the labor market. Employers are reluctant to take on someone in later life, knowing that they can be sued for discrimination if they let such people go before 70. There is, of course, legislation against age discrimination in hiring; but with many people competing for available jobs, it is very difficult, and often expensive and time consuming, for older women to document the fact that they have not been hired solely because of age.

While the style today is for young mothers to continue working, many of today's older women had their families in a time when it was the norm to be at home. In many cases they have very little work experience to offer. Though their instincts are careerist, fulfillment is difficult.

According to the 1976 Department of Labor, Women's Bureau publication, *Mature Women Workers: A Profile*, in 1975 nearly one third of all women workers were 45 years of age or over, a dramatic rise since 1950. Labor-force participation has been particularly pronounced for older married women.

Mature married women, however, are still less likely to be working than mature women who are widowed, divorced, or separated, because they encounter many obstacles in the job market as they seek to enter or reenter the labor force. They often find employers unwilling to credit their previous work experience or their activities during the period they were out of the labor force as evidence of future potential. Consequently, with the rusty or outmoded job skills, little or no recent experience, inadequate counseling, or a lack of job contacts, they frequently must settle for low-skilled and low-paying jobs which require little or no specialized training, and which afford limited opportunity for upward mobility.

These entry or reentry difficulties are reflected in mature women's occupational status and earnings, in the incidence of poverty, and in the duration of their unemployment. On the other hand, once mature women obtain jobs, they have a lower incidence of unemployment than younger women (p. 1).

There is some hope that the situation will improve for older careerists, although not immediately. Some economists have predicted that the aging of the society and the drop in the numbers of young people mean that in ten years there will be increased need for older people in the work force. These demographic changes may help older women in the future, but this is slight comfort to those now unemployed.

Ageism and Sexism

However, even those older women who are working are likely to be poor because women on the average earn 60 percent as much as men and because 90 percent of women workers are concentrated in more poorly paid occupations (see table 3).

The problem of retirement benefits for women who have left the labor market temporarily to raise children, as well as other inequities of social security, were well documented by Tish Sommers at the Economics of Aging conference in August 1975.

Table 3
Earnings of Fully Employed Men and Women by Race, 1965 and 1975

		1965	1975
Men	*White*	$6,704	$13,216
	....		
	Minority*	$4,277	$10,168
Women	*White*	$3,991	$7,614
	....		
	Minority*	$2,816	$7,505

*Includes all races other than white
Source: Prepared by the Women's Bureau, Employment Standards Administration, U.S. Department of Labor, from data published by the Bureau of the Census, U.S. Department of Commerce, August 1977.

At present no credit is given for the years of homemaking, and inflation makes many older women newly poor when they reach retirement.

In addition to job scarcity or loss of jobs because of ageism and low wages and retirement benefits, women careerist have a problem men usually do not have. If they are married, they usually do all or practically all of the homemaking in addition to their paid job. This gets harder as the woman ages. Older men get domestic services from wives, but older women careerists are usually the domestic servants too. Many women careerists joke that they need wives.

But even those able to get work and keep it experience certain difficulties because they are both older and female. Women in so-called men's fields or positions are sometimes lonely and segregated. If single, they do not fit into the coupled social activities stemming from work. At the same time, they are usually excluded from all-male lunch, drinking, poker, and other gatherings. They are thus also excluded from much of the politicking to advance careers that goes on at such gatherings.

Women in academic life, the professions, and business often find themselves shut out of the "old boy" networks where one gets sponsorship and other help. Out of necessity and loneliness, many women have started "old girl" networks. Arlene Kaplan Daniels of Northwestern University started a national organization for women sociologists, Sociologists for Women in Society. Now at conventions the women have their cronies. Several years ago Boston-area women started a Boston affiliate of Sociologists for Women in Society, and the chapter draws women from all the New England states. The same phenomenon has occurred in other professions.

Boston-area women psychiatrists found it necessary to start a support-discussion group of their own, even though the area is loaded with psychiatric organizations. Women throughout the country are grouping for support as even assertive women find many impediments to career development. For example, a weekend conference for professional women, "Managing Life Space," was held in Wentworth, New Hampshire, in October 1978. It attracted 50 careerists from all over the country, who spent $300 plus travel costs to hear how some famous career women manage their lives and to get support from each other. The conference was arranged by a husband-and-wife team of Protestant ministers, Elizabeth and David Dodson Gray, as part of their wider ministry. As a result of the conference, an ongoing group was set up among those from the Boston area.

Rebuffed or discounted by males they encounter in workplaces, many careerists get help and social relations from women associates. The women's movement has contributed to this development by emphasizing sisterhood rather than competitiveness or resentment among women. Nowadays you rarely hear from women that common old saw of the pre-sixties—"I would never work for a woman boss."

Professional women often need the kinds of reciprocity and interactions with women they get from the support groups because their male colleagues are sexist and less interested than most women in humanistic aspects of the delivery of service and working conditions. For instance, older women professors are frequently insulted, put down, and ignored by male colleagues because of disagreement over delivery of service to clients—in this case, the students.

The conflict of women's nurturant values with men's less humane ones has been most frequently demonstrated by the tensions between nurses and physicians. Nurses' desires to provide good patient care are frequently frustrated by the procedures and policies laid down by the men who control most hospitals. The fate of nurses' professionalism and their desire to exercise control consistent with their training and responsibility was movingly demonstrated in a hospital study carried out by Frances Portnoy. Some remarkable older nurses were severely punished for their attempts to provide good patient care, in opposition to the expedient policies of the male administrators and physicians who spent little time on the floors and had much less knowledge of daily operation than the nurses did. The physcian's assistant movement, in which P.A.'s are controlled by M.D.'s, is often considered to be an attempt by male physicians to head off the nurse practitioner movement, which gives highly trained and experienced nurses more autonomy, prestige, and rewards than they have traditionally been accorded.

Nursing is often seen as the prototype of sexual division of labor; most physicians consider women nurses handmaidens and do not allow them to use even one fourth of what they learn in good schools of nursing. Thus as nurses age, they cannot easily grow in knowledge and skill. Women in many other fields experience similar, if less visible discrimination.

While running a retirement workshop for the National Association of Manufacturers, I was not surprised to hear that a woman personnel officer was unable to get men executives to come to her preretirement planning programs. The male personnel officers reported some resistance but were generally able to get attendees from executive ranks. Sadly, but realistically, I suggested that she ask the highest-ranking male in the department to sign the invitations; chauvinism was clearly making males reject a program organized by a woman.

No matter how successful they are, older women careerists, like other older women, do not escape outright discrimination and the minor annoyances of being placed in an unequal, often disliked category. Promotions are slower. They get less pay often because, though they do the same work as men, the job titles are different. As one woman employment counselor said: "When I suggest a woman for a job, the salary offer suddenly drops." Moreover, women doing the same work as men do not get the same amount of secretarial help; they are frequently expected to be their own secretaries. Many highly ranked women even report that male colleagues ask them to type and do errands for them. As pointed out in Chapter 3, many older women are trained to respond helpfully and are likely to help out when asked. But as more women become assertive and refuse to do these chores, males accustomed to having women oblige them get a nasty shock, and they are not always good natured about the change.

There are, of course, exceptional males. When a woman finally rebelled at doing more than her share of routines, her male supervisor said: "Oh, you mean you don't want to be exploited?" However, this response came only after she sent him a long memo documenting the inequities and followed it up with a patient verbal explanation. It is worth noting that she could do this only because she had job security.

The Satisfactions and Sadness of Careerists

It would be endless and tedious to repeat here the many gripes careerist women have about sexist practices at work. These complaints have been well documented elsewhere. However, what is not commonly realized is the exhaustion and anxiety older women often experience in getting the ordinary services they need to function well in their jobs. For example, older women in areas dependent on cab transportation are often unable to get them; many drivers, themselves in economic stress, consider older women cranky and poor tippers. One woman told a meeting that she is forced to leave her car at the airport while on business trips even though garaging is more expensive than taking a cab.

Though careerists women can now get relief by sharing their complaints and seeking solutions together, not all women careerists are part of networks. Some seem to do well as loners—people have different needs and defenses. Older women careerists in happy marriages or other arrangements often get their reinforcement and interaction at home.

Doris, for example, who is about 50, doesn't tell her age; she is very capable and physically attractive. She is all business at work and doesn't "waste time with yacking around." She brings a sandwich for lunch, and eats at her desk rather than go to the cafeteria. She never gets involved with men at the office—she finds her lovers elsewhere.

Other women careerists find enough gratification and social interaction in their work and say they do not mind that there is no sexual intimacy in their lives. At least, they feel, there are sufficient compensations for its lack. Joan, a woman of 50, described her situation.

I was divorced when the children were young. I was very busy with the responsibility of taking care of them and working part time too. At that time, men would have complicated my relationship with my children and my life. When the kids left home, I lived alone for the first time and began to feel quite lonely. I did have one brief relationship with a man, but it was not very satisfying. What I did to make my life fuller was to get a new job – one that offered more challenge. In this job I am working with very bright people of both sexes. We go out to lunch together, and I travel for the company with other people. I work very hard and I am rewarded for my work. This feels good. I know celibacy is not considered terrific. In fact, for a long time, I thought there was something the matter with me because I did not run around looking for men. What I suffered from most was not sexual deprivation but the feeling that I somehow wasn't doing what I should. But I have got over that guilt trip – that there was something wrong with me – and I am enjoying my work, my woman friends, and managing without sex, thank you.

Some older women have moved out of social service jobs, which tend to burn out and under-reward their occupants. In jobs in the profit sector they have found satisfaction and the better pay with which to buy such niceties as vacations, insurance, good housing, and personal luxuries. They have also found the same rewards fortunate men find – a feeling of competence and opportunity. These older women, single and married, seem to handle the stresses of the work as well or as badly as their male counterparts. What angers them is that in many cases they must prove their professionalism to males and even to themselves. One reports: "The first few months on the job, I kept falling into that woman thing – oh, aren't I making mistakes, aren't I a klutz. It took me a while to realize that the men weren't going around agonizing about their mistakes, and they made plenty too. Finally, I learned to keep my mouth shut about my mistakes and mention my successes."

Older women careerists, no matter how successful, still grimace to hear men call them "sweetie" or "honey" and seek to infantilize them. They must continually remind people they are women not "girls."

Obviously, careerists, like other women, have other roles. As was emphasized in the introduction, the types used here are constructs for analysis. Careerists also may be nurturers; indeed, the creativity that goes into much work is not very different from the creativity of motherhood. In fact, one of the tragedies of our society is that we ask women to subordinate work creativity to family creativity and men to do the reverse. Both sexes are capable of nurturance and usually need to express their nurturant capacities in work and in loving reciprocal relationships: When Freud, who is wrongly believed to have been obsessed with sex, was asked at the end of his life what was important in life, he replied *lieben und arbeiten* –"loving and working."

When I was writing this book, I absorbed myself in it completely for a while and did nothing but take care of my bodily needs, listen to the news, answer the phone reluctantly, and get a bit of fresh air and exercise. As I followed this regimen, I had a sense of déjà vu, which I could not explain until one day I realized what process was being repeated. When each of my three infants was born, I had devoted almost all my time in the first few months to taking care of them in the same manner. Everything had revolved around them.

Any exciting work is as demanding as a newborn child. It is as thrilling for some women to watch a business grow as it was for me to see this book grow. Sadly, only about 3 percent of American businesses are owned by women; besides a lack of capital, there is an antipathy to business ingrained by socialization.

Many things indoctrinate women. The successful women

executive we described earlier said that she didn't intend not to marry; it just happened. Perhaps men thought her too competent. So young women, seeing that certain successful older women never marry are afraid they might always be alone, and draw back from career advancement at crucial stages. They fear they will lose out in the marriage market if they are more successful than eligible men or too busy to chase them. They know about older women like Natalie.

Natalie is an AUTHORITY. Her lecture fee is high because a good audience usually turns out to hear her. When it gets late, out of consideration for Natalie, the chairpersons stop the questions from the audience. Their concern is misplaced, but few in the audience, except the other older women, realize that Natalie is in no hurry to leave; she is happiest when she is on the platform. She is like the toys in the nursery tale who only come to life when the children play with them. When the lecture is over, Natalie will go home alone to her empty apartment or hotel room. She tries to keep her schedule as full as possible. When she is alone she always has the radio or television on, or she phones someone.

There are many successful career women like Natalie. Usually they carry calendar notebooks with pages jammed full of appointments, things to do, lists, and people they must call. An empty page must be filled in as soon as possible. But because of the occupational and social discrimination against them, there is less to put in that notebook as the years go by. Most older women get fewer requests, invitations, and other goodies. Younger women know this and sometimes can't bear to look at older women. They too frequently reject them, not wanting to see such unhappy models of their future.

One of the principal gratifications that older careerists have is the feeling that they do good work. But these days some men spoil the glow by telling women they are only getting ahead because of preferential treatment and affirmative action. Socialized to feel inadequate, women too often accept the barb. They ask: "Did I get the job or promotion because I was the only available woman?" "Did they give me the grant because they had to have a token woman?" "Am I taking the job away from a needy man, as the men say I am?" "Are they publishing my book because they need a woman author this year or a book about women, or is it really a good book?"

We never stop asking the kinds of questions men never think to ask. To get ahead, we have to be better than they are, work harder, never let down, and also do the laundry and smell nice. Yet, we do not trust ourselves because we have, despite our efforts, not completely unlearned those childhood lessons of inferiority and guilt. We hope it will be simpler for our daughters. We keep remembering that Margaret Mead said it was easier for her to be a career woman because her grandmother was one. So we try our best, in addition to struggling for ourselves, to be good role models to younger women. It is a heavy burden especially when they are clawing at us from below, as a woman professor, reports:

My students seem happy, my classes are crowded and my anonymous ratings are good. Yet two years ago a young male colleague, who is not as well liked by students as I am, suggested that maybe it was time at 50 for me to stop teaching because, after all, there were not any slots so he could advance. He is sure right; there are tragically more good Ph.D.'s around in most fields than jobs. I feel sorry for him and in fact spend a lot of time helping younger colleagues—male and female. However, does my status as an older woman automatically make me expendable and a target? The worst part of the story is that he actually made me feel guilty for a few minutes that I was taking up a job. Yet I do well and I am self-supporting and even help my adult kids and others a bit.

Older career women are very vulnerable to outside carping as well as to their own latent nurturance and feelings of inferiority and guilt. Yet, in spite of these and other problems, they manage. They are, indeed, the envy of many of the seekers described in the next chapter. Although they can't always get it, careerists, to a point, at least know what they want. Seekers usually do not.

CHAPTER SIX

Seekers

SEEKERS are discontented older women who believe happiness will at last be theirs if they buy or join, think new thoughts, or make some other change in their usually disappointing lives. They constantly seek to alter themselves, their possessions, and the environment. They move a great deal, either geographically, ideologically, or stylistically, always hoping the change will make life fuller and better.

Some seekers grasp at material things. They are to be found in stores and at rummage sales buying each others' discards, hoping to find the perfect item to transform themselves or their homes. They are after metamorphosis and hope to get it at a bargain. Garage sales and secondhand shops have multiplied, thanks to inflation, mobility, and seekers of both sexes and all ages. However, older women, the poorest aggregate, are especial habitués. It's all they can afford. Jay is fairly typical:

A never-married woman of 56, Jay has a regular route of secondhand clothing stores. She is constantly changing sizes because of weight fluctuations. When she is depressed, she puts on weight; when things go well, which is rarely, she loses. Her weight swings are also tied to the income she makes selling encyclopedias on commission. When sales are good, she eats protein and salads; when times are tougher she consumes a lot of bread, cereal, and cheap candy. It is in the "fat" off season that she roams the shops, looking for something to make her feel and look better. Jay thinks that if she looks better she will sell more encyclopedias. Often she finds something that pleases her and gets excited about it. Once it is in the closet, however, she frequently loses interest in it. Jay feels her life is pretty empty and sometimes thinks buying other peoples' clothes is like buying part of someone's happier life. In the same way, Jay copies the hairstyles of women she envies.

Barbara is another seeker. At 50 she has been divorced for five years, and her three children are now independent. Her husband got the house, which was near his business, and she got a cash settlement. Barbara mourned the loss of the house where she had expected to entertain her grandchildren. But she felt better when she found an attractive apartment in the city and she spent a lot of time, effort, and money fixing it up. Once it was finished, however, she became disappointed with it. She found a way to break the lease in six months and rented a small suburban house.

As soon as the year lease was up, Barbara moved again, this time into an apartment complex with a swimming pool. Then this seeker decided she would never be happy until she again owned her own home; so she quickly bought a small cottage. When she decided it was too expensive and lonely and started to look for a large co-op house, she found that she had paid more for the cottage than she could sell it for. Her running from depression had proven expensive. Depression caught up with her when she was too exhausted and financially depleted to run.

Restless older women like Barbara delight real estate brokers. Many older women have complained of exploitative landlords and realtors. Not unusual is the agent who found an apartment for a new widow and collected fees from both her and the landlord. Another widow reported: "I carefully explained in great detail to realtors exactly what I wanted. Top priority was a quiet street away from a major highway. Small and one floor and fairly new was also essential. I know how to convey information. I'm a schoolteacher. But it was as if I had never spoken. Though realtors listened, and some even wrote down what I said, they insisted on driving me to every large white elephant on major highways. Until I found an older woman agent, I was houseless."

Many people seem to think older women are deaf, blind, or at least gullible. Sadly, it is true that some women are inexperienced in business dealings, and during stressful transitions seekers may be so desperate that their judgment is blurred.

There are, of course, seekers who could never own houses or have any valuable possessions. They are the poorest women, the ones you sometimes see picking up things from the gutter, trash cans, or dumps. There is always the hope they will find a treasure to enrich them or at least to pay for dinner. Some poor seekers have regular routes and are well known and tolerated as neighborhood curiosities.

Of course, students also salvage items out of trash cans, but for students poverty is transitional; older women seekers have little hope of outgrowing their need for these habits. For them survival is always problematic.

Less economically deprived older women, driven by misery, hope, curiosity, boredom, and other motivations, experiment with the procession of popular fads, such as new therapies and religions. Some have enriched charlatans with their energy, ideas, and money, while others have contributed to constructive new movements.

Seeking Experience

In the absence of other possibilities, seekers are the natural prey of opportunists—none of whose hearts really bleed for older women.

In the discussion of unutilized nurturers I criticized inadequate, though sometimes well-meaning therapists. Seekers also suffer from such people and from other not-so-well-meaning individuals and organizations. Traveling a circuit of fortune tellers, astrologers, "psychics," and clairvoyants of various sorts, seekers exchange accolades about their finds and flock to the latest celebrities on the hope list. They are delighted to be understood; they do not realize that their sorrows and hopes are so common that it is easy for those they patronize to describe them. Some seekers may find hope or harmless diversion at a price and suffer no bad effects. Others, like Renée, may have a very destructive experience:

At age 40, Renée was bored with her job. She thought, "There must be more to life than being a receptionist." She knew her boss wanted a younger woman at the front desk and felt humiliated. He was always telling her, "You're not as young as you used to be." She agreed that if he fired her, she would not protest. That way she would get severance pay, collect unemployment compensation, and have a long time to "find out who I am," as she put it. She decided to do this because of a magazine ad for a "spiritual retreat center" run by Yogi Something. It was expensive, considering the vegetarian food, but Renée paid in advance for three months and sublet her apartment. She was surprised to find she had to help cook the vegetarian food, mostly starches, in a hot kitchen. It was uncomfortable sleeping on a cot in a room with six other people and no screens on the windows. But, as she told her friends, "There were a lot of laughs, especially when we were all running to the john from the damn dire-rear." She came home too thin, with a trace of scurvy around the lips and a back sore from yoga positions to find that the students to whom she had sublet had ruined her furniture. She was annoyed that Yogi's disciples kept calling for months afterward, asking for donations and help in recruiting other retreaters.

Renée tried out a few other renewal movements and then decided to become an author. "I felt that by writing I could get myself together and earn." She paid for a writers' correspondence course out of the last of her savings, but she found it very hard to make herself write and began to get severely depressed staying home. She finally decided to forget authorship and seek a new job.

She had worked since the age of eighteen and had a great deal of experience, so it was a terrible shock to find out that employers didn't want her. Finally she discovered that her former boss was giving poor references. Having worked hard there for fifteen years, she was very angry. She called to ask why this knifing. He answered: "You behaved like an adolescent. Anyone who didn't have the sense to hold on to a good job working for me, I can't recommend." She ended up working as a temporary clerical at lower pay than she had earned before.

Not all older explorers get into this much difficulty. Some improve their lives by new experiences. Unfortunately, however, a number of older women are seduced into injudicious seeking, spinning their wheels too long and too expensively.

New widows and divorcées have long been recognized as good prey, and now there are faddy swindlers to sell shoddy "salvation" as well as the more traditional shoddy merchandise. A sad widow, Sandra, made the mistake of trying to distract herself by dropping into a so-called church. Here is her story:

I had seen the sign on the nice-looking building for a long time. Since Joe died, I look for things to do. So I dropped in one day and a nice-looking young couple there gave me booklets and seemed pleased to see me. They talked to me for hours about their beliefs. It was pleasant to be with these young people instead of alone in my apartment or just walking around. Then they explained how much it would cost to get "neonated," which is what they mean by feeling relieved of things troubling you. I was shocked that it was such a large sum—hundreds of dollars—and I immediately decided not to get involved. I said goodbye and left.

Imagine my surprise the next day when the bell rang at my home. Those two young people had taken a long bus ride to see me. I felt very embarrassed that they had any indication I was that interested; they made me feel as if I had led them on. It is a good thing I couldn't spare the money or I might have felt obligated to take the "neonated" business. They kept calling later to see if I could afford it. They are damn pests, but I did get up their hopes, I guess.

Made polite in their childhoods, older women are often no match for assertive true believers or charlatans of various sorts. Poor or needing help themselves, they may be induced to give to the seeming poor or helpful. Seeking better lives, they often fall into the hands of those more determined and greedier than themselves. And still, like Sandra, they may think they are somehow obligated.

Some middle- and upper-class women have a good time test-
ing all the latest whatevers. It is a lark, and they have enough
money to indulge in this hobby. "What's Ma (or Aunt Sara) into
now?" everyone wants to know. Occasionally, such women discover something worthwhile that adds to their lives and even en-
riches others. But sometimes they get burned. The trouble is that
the least-educated, most vulnerable women with the most to lose
seem to get hurt worst. They don't explore as intelligently and in
as limited a way as more fortunate women, precisely because
those with less education and resources are so desperate to have
something interesting or fulfilling in their lives. The same older
woman who a few years ago might have gotten vicarious excitement from watching soap operas now wants more. And there are
people to sell it to her. What she frequently learns is that older
women often get exploited.

Seeking Education

Nothing is sacred or always ethical. Even in going back to school,
seekers need to be careful.

Lena is newly separated, with little money. At 40, she knew
she had at least twenty-five work years ahead. She didn't want to
be dependent on her kids. She had married young and waitressed
part-time while raising her family. She did not look forward to
another twenty-five years of waiting on tables, and besides her
feet hurt. A friend suggested that she go back to school, so she
looked on the education page of the Sunday paper and saw an ad
for a hotel management course. The ad said there were jobs waiting with excellent pay. Lena figured she would be good at that
work because she had run a home and waitressed in hotels. The
tuition was high but Lena saw it as an investment in her future.
Besides, the director of admissions of the proprietary (profitmaking) school was very persuasive.

Her internship turned out to be hotel waitressing at lower
wages than she had made before. The courses themselves were

shoddy. When the year was up and she asked the school for a management placement, they gave her a list of area hotels and the names of the personnel directors. They also told her that she had done poorly in the courses, and they really didn't see how they could recommend her as they had many bright young people to place.

Lena did not know that she could have complained to the state regulatory authorities or that she could have taken cheaper courses and gotten some guidance on what to study at her local community college. Of course, there is no certainty that she would have been advised properly there, nonprofit though it was. Many an older woman has spent much time and money at a good college preparing for jobs that are already glutted with applicants in her community. If she is tied to the area, because of marriage or for other reasons, she is out of luck. Often, out of self-interest, conscious or unconscious, even ethical educational institutions advise students to enroll in programs in which the schools have heavy investment and resources—even though the programs will not lead to jobs.

Nonetheless, seeking life change through education can be constructive and successful for older women. Some educational returnees have made good choices and done well, becoming careerists or advocates as a result. Education can become role therapy, and many women undergo remarkable transformations late in life. There is often pain in the process, for any change involves giving up old ways of thinking and behaving, and this is not easy. In addition, administrators and faculty, with notable exceptions, are not always attuned to the needs and problems of older returning students.

In my study of older women returnees for the Boston University graduate school I discovered that for many the flight to education was from disintegrating marriages and finances or from boredom and depression after children no longer required full-time mothering. I also found that though women experienced considerable anxiety in educational institutions, they nevertheless did well academically. On the whole they succeeded remarkably well in achieving their goals of role transformation.

Some innovations in education may provide programs suited to better meet the needs of returnees. In 1978 the Association of American Colleges received a QUILL grant from the Ford Foundation, the projects funded included plans to integrate liberal learning with career and professional education and to strengthen the liberal learning component of continuing education.

The Bureau of Labor Statistics pamphlet, *Going Back to School at 35 and Over* by Anne McDougall Young, reports that in October 1976 1.6 million persons 35 years and over were enrolled in school, a 100,000 increase since October 1974. The report notes that "almost all of the increase has occurred among white unmarried women. Most of these women are self-supporting and many regard further education as necessary for career development. All of the increase in school enrollment has been at the college undergraduate level." The pamphlet reports that in all, 958,000 American women over 35 were in school in 1976. Of these, 622,000 were married with a husband present, and 336,000 had another marital status. The 35-to-39-year-olds numbered 296,000; the 40-to-44-year-olds, 213,000; the 45-to-49-year-olds, 147,000; and those fifty years and over, 302,000.

Of the women attending school 65 percent were also in the labor force. Of the 958,000 women over 35 less than 5 percent were below the college level. Trade or vocational schools accounted for 22 percent. Fifty-eight percent were college graduates and 15 percent graduate students.

Now that there is a drop in the number of young students for admission, many colleges formerly unreceptive to older students are courting them. It is very important that tragedies such as that of Lena be averted by proper routing of returnees. Although in most places scholarships are available only for full-time students, the Bureau of Labor Statistics figures indicate that most women returnees must work while attending school. Since their pay is usually low, they must strain to pay for courses. Part-time scholarships, badly needed by such women, are now very rare.

Sound, disinterested advice is also a scarce commodity in most areas. For older women, seeking financial advice can be hazardous. Many older women do not know how to make the most of their usually limited incomes or how to invest earned or inherited money. Fortunately, many organizations and schools are now giving programs in money management for older women. Unfortunately, some of the people giving these courses are not entirely disinterested. Investment teachers and counselors may try to sell students costly services or poor investments.

On all fronts, more reliable referral centers and better options than now prevail are needed by seekers. Too many get hurt. Compassion is in short supply generally in this society, and many hostile or opportunistic people feel that older women deserve what they get—or don't get. The same mentality that forgives rapists for being provoked by clean and attractive women figures that older women, ravished of money or hopes by charlatans, had it coming to them. We do little about consumer protection or protection for older seekers. Had Sandra been "neonated" expensively, she would have been considered a fool in many quarters, just as Lena was considered "a dumb broad" for taking a fraudulent hotel course. It is easy to denigrate older women. Educating and protecting them takes a share of society's interest and resources.

Eternal Seekers

Although for many older women, seeking is a transitional state, for others it becomes a permanent way of life. They remain eternal seekers, always on the outside wishing to be inside but prevented either by rejection, finances, skepticism, or other factors. That very marginality that drives them to seeking can prevent

the desired immersion and integration in something that would
bring about the real change they desire. Where they most seek to
be included, they are often excluded by poverty or a paired world.
The more critical they are, the less they can settle for groups or
causes of low rationality or status. Intellectuality may add to
their choices but also to their ambivalence and aloneness. Competent women not only threaten men; they also find it hard to locate
social units to which they can belong anywhere.

Selena, whose seeking drove her to several psychotherapists,
told the following story:

*It was one of those awful lonely Saturdays. I went to a couple of flea
markets, garage sales, and hit the stores' sales. Then I just didn't
want to go home for Saturday night alone, even though I had a lot
of papers to correct for my high school students. I just sort of drove
around aimlessly. Then I saw a small, fundamentalist church with
a lot of people going in for what must have been a revival meeting.
Suddenly, although I have been an atheist all my life, I wanted to
go in with them. I had a fantasy of being baptized and them all
embracing me and inviting me into their lives and community. I
was ready to embrace Jesus, to be embraced by those people. But of
course I did not actually do it.*

Selena did, however, experiment with a whole series of intel-
lectual esoteric movements in a vain attempt to find a comfortable ideology. She found fanatics who amused or annoyed her and
shifting or coupled memberships that did not give her the sense of
community she needed. So she continued seeking indefinitely,
hoping to change herself so that she could fit someplace. In the
meantime, she finds her community in paid friendship with
therapists.

There are a few older women who have enough money to seek
throughout the world. Their money can buy them diversion and
paid escorts, even lovers. Instead of garage sales or McDonald's,
they patronize haute couture and haute cuisine. They are sometimes envied and often ridiculed. But what they really seek, they

usually do not find because, like other older women, they are not really respected. Cosmetic surgery may make them more attractive by cruel, youth-inspired standards; but the frenetic jet-set pace usually palls and these women become justly suspicious of the opportunistic fawning they receive. With older female seekers of various statuses, it is often trite but nevertheless true that "anybody that would want me, I would not want."

Older women who have relinquished the hope of finding male companionship often turn elsewhere to fill the intimacy void. Thus, unutilized nurturers are also in a sense seekers, looking for a way to re-engage in nurturance or in something that will give focus to their lives. In early stages they may be exploited because they volunteer and work hard in order to become involved and valued. Later, they may become disillusioned and either seek elsewhere or change to another pattern, such as faded beauties or chronic patients.

Certainly many seekers find their causes, are happy with them, and become advocates and assertive older women. Many have found a place as feminists, antifeminists, or in political camps.

What has been said here is not meant to negate the value of seeking. All of us need to seek better social arrangements for our society. All unhappy persons should be seeking; but they have to exercise caution in this process. Better guidelines are needed. The drive older women have toward something better in their lives is understandable in view of their circumstances. But can we help them find something better than old clothes, shoddy houses, utopias, and mis-education? These women have capabilities that would flourish with genuine options and good direction. The trouble is that neither their needs nor their capabilities are respected, and too many seek in vain. Disillusioned, many go on to adopt some of the more unfortunate roles discussed in the next few chapters.

CHAPTER SEVEN

Faded Beauties

ANOTHER KIND of seeking that characterizes older women is the search for beauty – a search usually doomed to fail because the eyes of most beholders have a passion for youth. Many feminist writers have already described how women have been socialized to develop their appearance and nurture it in a losing battle with the double standard of aging by which women are labeled old and "shelved" at an earlier age than men.

The faded beauty fights her demise with beauty salons, cosmetics, diets, plastic surgery, clothes, health clubs, and sometimes reassurance from lovers. As she fades, she may help the economy by consuming products and services that promise youth. However, her consumption is usually thwarted by her shrinking income or time.

Faded beauties are often satirized. Yet such women are correct in their belief that the society generally rejects older women, whose sex-symbol and mothering functions are things of the past. It is difficult to redirect the aspirations and motivations of faded beauties; theirs is an intense disappointment in men and in a society that passes on the laurel to new beauties. Such women don't know any other ways to gain status. "Your face is your fortune my pretty maid" we are taught.

Older women, taking heroic, expensive, and often futile measures to appear young are the target of many jokes and of advertisers. The jokes and ads are as sick as the age-phobic culture that produces them. For instance, on February 11, 1978, a radio newscaster said: "Today is actress Kim Stanley's fifty-third birthday, but don't tell anyone I told you." It is as if it is shameful to get older.

Many older women dye their hair, though they would rather not, to get or keep a job or a man. Indeed one haircoloring was touted in an advertisement as absolutely essential "if you want to go back to work now that your children are grown." Unfortunately the ad is probably true, for there is job discrimination against older persons. Surveys have shown that grayness is, for most respondents, the greatest indicator of age. Older urbanites of both sexes have reported they dye their hair because the gray haired, who are thought to be weaker, are more frequently mugged.

There was a great deal of concern and anger among older women in 1978 when it was reported that hair-coloring products advertised as necessary to their success were possibly cancer-causing. When asked about the possible risk, some women said flatly: "I'll keep dyeing – I don't want to find out how gray I am." Others repressed their anxiety. The women were torn between their fear of cancer and a greater fear of rejection by self and others. One interviewee reported that, when a new permanent had stripped the color out of her hair and it could not be dyed again immediately, she would not leave the beauty parlor until dark. She became a recluse until her hair was recolored. If you think such women vain or foolish, consider the following incident. It occurred at a meeting of divorced, widowed, and never-married persons organized by a minister as a self-help group.

Marjorie, an attractive widow of forty-three, asked plaintively, "Why do men who are my age want to date my daughter and why are the only men who want to date me the age of my mother?" The half dozen men in the room did not respond, but the two dozen women all nodded emphatically. (There are almost always more women than men at such groups.) After a strained period of silence, Mary, another attractive mid-life woman, turned to the men and asked: "Do you *all* prefer much younger women?" They all nodded yes except one man who was past sev-

enty; he said he prefers women "about my age." Mary then
turned to Joe and asked him to tell her why he preferred younger
women? "I just do. I can't tell you why." Silence again descended!
Finally, another man rescued Joe by saying "younger women
have more energy and are better dancers," and other men nodded
in agreement. A lively 60-year-old woman piped up: "I love to
dance and can dance all night—I never get tired and I'm a good
dancer." The men didn't seem to hear her, or at least they didn't
respond. The topic of conversation was changed by one of the men.

The attitudes of those men are quite common, discouragingly
so. In the ads in *Single Booklovers* and other such matchmaking
listings, almost all men request contact with women ten to twenty
years younger than themselves; and they may be lying about
their own age. (Most people past 30 in America shave off a few
years.) For many women, panic comes as early as 30 with the first
wrinkle, breast sag, gray hair, or double-edged remark that "it
makes you look younger, dear."

In this book, I have deliberately avoided saying at what age
one becomes an older woman. This is because the age varies when
one is defined by others or defines oneself. But in general, self-defi-
nition as "old" lags substantially behind society's definition.
Faded beauties especially deny their age because they have come
to depend upon audiences.

In the early days of radio, many humor shows failed until
they brought in studio audiences to respond to the actors and, by
responding, encourage them to be funny. Human beings, except
for a few hermits, take their cues from those around them. We
look to others to tell us who we are. So, by 40, the crisis of 30
hardens into a chronic condition for many women who depend on
admiration from men to tell them they have what they want
most—desirability.

Part of the problem is that life has made these women too
wise, as well as too dry of skin. Men in mid-life crisis do not want
women who have traveled with them along what now seems a
dead-end and unsatisfactory road. They hope to affiliate them-

selves with a younger cohort through younger women and thus get a second chance at happiness. Many feel that responsibilities robbed them of their youth and that it is not too late to recoup. Being with younger women allows them to deny aging somewhat. Moreover, women their own age know about their clay feet and past failures; younger women look up to them.

Of course, many marriages survive, or do not experience, the mid-life itch. Not all men roam. Indeed some older marriages are revitalized; in many, love deepens. But some ex-beauties deeply resent their husbands' obvious fascination with unwrinkled faces and firm breasts, taking it as a derogation of their own bodies and devotions. Most wives are deeply wounded when husbands prop up their egos with affairs, casual, sustained, or even fantasized.

The depth of the wound and its repairability depends on the wife's ego, values, and her options. Some women with limited financial and emotional resources feel they have little choice but to ignore such slights, especially when children are still being educated. Some read *Playboy* with their husbands, are titilated, and also resocialized by it. They accept new values and may begin to experiment.

Interestingly enough, wives who complain to advice columns are usually told to forgive their mid-life and older men for their potency with other women or their impotency at home. Paradoxically women are often rejected by their mates just at the point when they have high sexual desire. One of the sad facts of older marriages is that when children are no longer draining them of energy, many women experience renewed sexual interest—just when their husbands, often older and tired, are less able to perform sexually. Fading beauties need and expect sexual attention, and their demands make some aging men anxious and angry. Defensively, they blame their wives for their sexual dysfunction, though such dysfunction is really a very complex outgrowth of two people's interactions and of social myths, stereotypes, and the frustrations that make mid-life men feel powerless and obsolete.

Some women, for whom male attention is paramount in life,

seek it extramaritally when rejected by their husbands. However, the same columnists or counselors who advise wives to save the marriage and forgive male infidelities or disinterest seldom suggest that older women get their satisfaction elsewhere. Forbearance and sublimation is recommended. Probably such advisers base their advice on more than morality. If they are practical and realistic they know that a wife past forty is hardly likely to find a substitute for the bored or erring husband – the sex ratio at later ages and the double standard of aging are against her. Also the angry wife who retaliates or looks for solace with lovers is much more apt to be criticized by her community than the husband who started the game. More sexual restraint is still expected of women, despite supposed changes in values. Too many statements on the new morality are based on urban coastal mores, not on middle America.

The unremarried divorcée, widow, or never-married older woman also frequently suffers continuous slights to her self-image as a desirable woman. Some voluntarily endure the frustration of celibacy because, as explained in earlier chapters, they are unwilling to settle for casual sex. But they would still like to be admired and, as they age, they usually are not. Faded beauty types find it almost unendurable that men no longer show even casual complimentary interest. A few become promiscuous to prove they are attractive to men, since, as girls they were never allowed to feel they had any other value. To faded beauties, work, nurturance, friendships with women, and hobbies have always been less important than their identity, experiences, and tribute as sex objects. Fading and the normal decrements of age are more traumatic for them than for other women. Those who are sexually active and permissive may find that their sex life declines with the years. If sexual relationships and approval from men had been the center of their lives, they experience great loss and pain.

One interviewee, a poet of 55, said she no longer wrote poetry because she could only write when she was in love and loved, and now nobody wanted her. In a less extreme way, other faded beauties lose their occupation and inspiration when men begin to ignore them.

Widows who have gained their chief gratification in life from being their husbands' sweethearts often see no meaning to life without male devotion. They need a man to tell them who they are. Late in life they find it hard to meet a new man, even if they are ready to do so. A 47-year-old widow, who was formerly very fastidious, explains: "When he died I could hardly bear to go on. I stopped caring how I looked. Sometimes I didn't clean the house, take a bath, or change my sheets or wash my hair for a month. Why should I? Who was there to see or smell? I stopped buying clothes, though I had enough money. My friends said I needed another man, and one tried to fix me up once with a widower 20 years older than me. He reminded me of my father. I feel now as if my life is over. Without anyone to keep myself up for, what is the sense of bothering?"

Other widows, also fading beauties, feel differently and primp for whatever audiences *are* available. If they cannot get compliments from men, at least they want other women and their children to tell them how nice they look. Even a grocery shopping expedition requires dressing up and careful grooming. People everywhere are mirrors for them. Sometimes they wear too much makeup, jewelry, and inappropriate clothes in an attempt to hide the fading.

Forty-year-old Stella found a minor incident traumatic. When furnishing her small apartment after her husband's death, she bought a lamp table in a small shop. It was not really too heavy for her to carry, but she asked the proprietor to put it in her car because she didn't want to hurt her troublesome back trying to fit it into the small trunk. As he wedged it in, she apologized for bothering him, explaining about her back. He answered: "Well, I have a bad back too, but at least I'm a lot younger than you." Immediately Stella aged ten years in her imagination. Clearly the man was at least her age, if not older, but she obviously looked ancient to him. She went home and colored her hair again. She never liked that table.

Though people see aging in others, it is more difficult to see or admit it in themselves. A divorced woman, Lisette, told me about her moment of truth:

My women friends got sick of hearing me say how much I hated being alone. They pushed me to join a certain club because they said there were a lot of single men there. There were a few, much to my delight. I looked around the table and saw two very attractive men and my hopes rose. I smiled, but they looked away. Suddenly, I realized they were probably in their late thirties, and there I was 50 years old. Somehow through the years I had never changed my image of the kind of man that turned me on. When I was married to Phil, he never seemed old to me – he changed so gradually, I guess.

Older women, like older men, have distorted self-conceptions and conceptions of others. The difference is that older women must make an adjustment that men can evade because men corner the buyers' market – for reasons already discussed. (Of course, there are men who like older women, and there is a small fad for them in certain limited quarters.)

Older women, who have as much need for sexual expression as other humans, endure in silence or vocalize their frustration to friends. One vocal, never-married faded beauty summed it up this way: "I haven't touched or been touched by a man for three years, since my steady boyfriend of ten years and I split. I've forgotten what sex is. At this point, if one asked me and he was clean, I would go to bed with him immediately, but I don't think one will come along and I'm not really sure that at the last minute I wouldn't chicken out. He might have V.D. or despise me later, and I have enough troubles."

Reinforcement of this woman's fears probably came from the experience of some of her friends. At a large sexuality workshop sponsored by a state-wide singles' club, several older women related that they had had sexual relations with men on the first date. They felt it was expected of them, and they also hoped to hold the men that way. In any case, they were, as they put it, "hungry for affection." The women reported that these dates turned out to be "one-night stands." One said: "I thought if I showed him how beautiful my body was, things would work out with him, but I never heard from him again."

The ambivalence many older women feel about casual sex adds to the reasons driving men into the arms of less conflicted young women, who grew up on different movies in the era of the pill. This may partly explain why the man at the singles' group refused to tell why he preferred younger women. For him, it may have been too strenuous to deal with the emotional needs of older women, who often need reassurance that they are still desirable. They also often need to feel that they are "good girls," for the morality pounded into their heads years ago troubles them still. Many older men are unwilling to cope with the tensions involved, especially when younger women are plentiful and, as they say, "make less of a big deal about sex." Men who do not care to marry or make a commitment admit that "it's too much of a hassle to get involved with a nice lady." Paying alimony or educating children, some feel unable to remarry in any case.

Older women's struggles over sexual decisions are illustrated by the experience of Rita, 51, who was recently divorced after a marriage of twenty-seven years to the only lover she had ever had:

Rita, with considerable self-doubt and anxiety, put an ad in a magazine "to correspond with a gentleman." She lived in a small town, and the only men she knew were other people's husbands. She was very disappointed when several months passed without any mail from the ad. A man-centered woman, she longed for romance and wept copiously and enviously when she saw lovers in the movies, on television, and even on the street. Finally, a letter came from a nice-sounding man who said he was flying to a city near her town on business in a few weeks. He asked if she would be willing to come into the city to have dinner or a drink with him. Rita started to write him to call her when he arrived figuring she would see how he sounded on the telephone. Then she decided it would be awful to be on tenterhooks waiting for his call. She reasoned that she could either call him long distance after 11:00 P.M. or before 8:00 A.M., when the rates were low. She decided to run the risk of waking him in the morning instead of at night, but when she called, a woman answered, and Rita hung up. Then, she felt foolish, realizing that, since he had put his phone number in the letter, he could not be married. He might live in a cooperative house or have a sister or a daughter. She began to agonize that, though she had never met him, she had a rival who had spent the night with him. After a while she decided not to call again but to write. However, she procrastinated so long about mailing the letter, that he could not have received it before he left home. She never met him. Ambivalence had triumphed.

Not all older women are so indecisive. Some are fleet at the chase in bars or elsewhere, and are envied or despised as cheap by slower and more inhibited women. However, some older women face unexpected discouragement; their hopes are raised by attractive, older, never-married, or divorced men. After investing energy and fantasy, they discover these men prefer bachelorhood, their mothers, or other men. "How was I to tell he was a homosexual?" women ask after pining and primping in vain. In other cases women now past 40 who were married when very young simply do not know how to deal with the mating-dating game. They feel like adolescents, and they resent this feeling. One woman made the mistake of seeking advice from her own 20-year-old daughter. The daughter said: "Ma, I don't care what you do, but I don't want to know when you do it."

A frequent topic at singles' clubs meetings is whether to let your children know about your sexual arrangements. Faded beauties who have the opportunity for a sexual liaison frequently are faced with the dilemma of the impact of actions on their adolescents' values and behavior. Some settle for deprivation; others, frankness or concealment. Such women look to the "experts" for advice, but those in the helping professions vary in response, and there is little solid research in this sensitive area.

A tragedy for many younger-older women is that while there are few truly eligible men, there are always bosses eager to pat or pinch or take more and retaliate if rejected. Phyllis, a beautiful 40-year-old administrative assistant, learned that her employer had engaged a single room when the two had to go to a meeting in another city. She told him as sweetly as she could: "I'll have dinner with you but I can't sleep with you." Obviously hurt, he asked, "why are you rejecting me. Don't you like me?" Trying to be tactful, Phyllis replied: "Of course, I like you, but I also like your wife. You have to go home to her. I have to see her."

The employer continued to insist that Phyllis was mean and cruel to turn him down. He assumed that because she was an older woman alone, she was desperate and fair game. After the trip, things were so uncomfortable that Phyllis reluctantly sought a new job. The worst part of the story was that she admitted to herself that her employer's offer was "the best I've had all year, and it was nice to know that I am still attractive. I needed that."

Stuck in unfulfilling work, Phyllis and many other older women would like to continue to achieve as beauty queen bees, which they were taught was all-important. Perhaps this teaching has not changed much; many of my young women students tell me that their mothers, aunts, grandmothers, and fathers keep asking "how is your social life?" rather than "how are you growing intellectually?" Though students try to reject this pressure, it sticks to them like glue. It makes them uneasy if they study too much and are not popular with men. They may never get rid of the feeling that this is the central issue in their lives. In the meantime, the Oil of Olay advertisements remind them that older womanhood will soon be upon them. They suspect cosmetics will not solve all the consequent problems and they are right.

There is no more pathetic sight than a health club full of older women sweating toward the dream of looking like the 20-

year-old instructors, svelte and nubile in their black leotards. No amount of sweat, massage, cream, or uncomfortable underclothing will undo those years of living. Disguises, like Halloween costumes, may help to go seeking treats, but tricks are always in the offing for older women. Faded beauties, the most youth-invested of all, often experience the most deprivation as they age.

Their emphasis on physical appearance and the body has a further ramification. Many become what I call doctorers; they convert their obsession with physical beauty into an obsession with health. The body that has betrayed them thus becomes the canvas upon which they express their psychic wounds. Desperate for attention, they get it where they can; it is sometimes painful and expensive, and it may injure the very health and beauty they wish to enhance. Their efforts will be discussed in the next chapter.

CHAPTER EIGHT

Doctorers

DOCTORERS are women for whom illness has become a life motif. The sick role replaces other roles lost or denied by circumstances, providing an occupation and a kind of status when other identities are not available. Being ill gains attention.

Health handicaps, either real or imagined, also provide the woman and those around her with an explanation for why she is not socially useful or desirable. Often older persons find it more psychologically comfortable to believe they are ill—and therefore cannot work or have good social interactions—than to admit that they are unwanted by society because they are aging.

Defining oneself as ill, therefore, can have multiple functions. It can gain attention from and punish those who are rejecting you. It can also create self-preoccupation that diverts one from feelings of loss.

Certainly not all doctorers are feigning illness. Many mid-life women are ill because of the stresses in their lives and the health hazards prevalent in modern society. Many do not get proper health care because of finances or because physicians consider their problems unsolvable or themselves nuisances. In fact, I call such women doctorers, rather than patients because some of them "doctor" themselves or are treated by other women or noncredentialed healers. Some have had bad experiences with physicians, cannot afford them, or find a more cordial reception elsewhere.

Though American women outlive men on the average by eight years, women are more often patients. This perplexing phenomenon is described by Robert Atchley in *The Social Forces in Later Life* (p. 130):

> Based on mortality we would expect older males to show high rates of physician visits, disability and hospitalization. In fact, the reverse is true. Older women show consistently higher rates of morbidity (illness) even if we take into account the fact that there are more women in the older population. This puzzling relationship between sex differences in illness and in deaths has not been satisfactorily explained, but its implications are clear: older women predominate among the sick, the older men predominate among the dead.

Before condemning older women for being doctorers, consider their often empty lives as described in earlier chapters. People readily admire, touch, and pet children, animals, and even inanimate objects but not, usually, older women. The tactile need is genuine. Touching and being touched is a part of human experience; the growth of the massage industry is not entirely due to its disguised advertising of sexual services. Nonerotic massages are ways for people who do not get touched to buy that comfort. Older women using amateur or professional masseuses are seeking, in perhaps the only way available to them, contact and attention. Similarly, the older woman who runs to doctors at every twinge, may be purchasing the only kind of touching or attention she can get. Partly it is a sexual sublimation and partly it is a simple demand for human contact and a hope for direction toward a better existence. As Arthur Miller said in *Death of a Salesman*, "Attention must be paid." In this case, it is also paid *for*, either by the woman or by third-party payments or government health expenditures.

That women seek medical reassurances when their lives are unhappy is consistent with the medicalization of American society, for Americans look to physicians to solve problems of living, even though the doctors often cannot solve these problems for themselves. This is partially because in our secular society physicians are the high priests. And in fact medicine has produced some dramatic successes in our era, although there is some disillusionment among older people who were brought up to expect science to solve all problems. Children learned at home, in school, and from the media that one should turn to the experts. Now in their older years, unhappy people turn to physicians as the highest of experts. They seek out the scientific medical care they have been promised as part of the American faith.

Sadly, they often seek in vain. Robert Butler, M.D., Director of the National Institute of Aging, has often stated that older persons are disproportionately subject to emotional and mental problems, and that about 80 percent of elderly people who need assistance will not get it—either for financial reasons, rejection by physicians, or because they are considered by themselves or others to be "just getting old."

Older women have seen that the elderly are neglected in our society. Is it any wonder then that in age-phobic America, many women become intense about preventing any further aging decrements than those they see in the mirror? Seeking health care may represent a realistic desire not to become disabled, but overzealous preoccupation with health may also mask feelings of being surplus people—feelings experienced especially by ex-nurturers, faded beauties, and unemployed careerists. Hypochondria is thus both a search for more vital options and a role for the roleless older woman.

However, it is important to understand that many older women are *not* hypochondriacs. They have real ailments that are neglected by the medical establishment. Too often, physicians stereotype and dismiss all older women as chronic complainers or menopausal or postmenopausal emotional casualities. Treatable conditions are overlooked. There is no women's circle without its horror stories of women told by physicians "it is just nerves; buy yourself a new hat" only to discover—perhaps too late—that there were serious physical problems. And the research bears out the folklore.

It is not that physicians are deliberately neglectful or unkind but that most medical education fails to prepare doctors to deal with the physical and emotional problems of older women. Busy physicians are frustrated and bored by the uninteresting conditions and lives of most older women. They generally do not know how to help them change their situations and often do not have or take the time to talk with such women. Sometimes they treat their miseries with the kind of belittling patronizing that drives the women to self-treatment or friendly quacks and therapies.

Drugs

One way busy physicians deal with the problems of older women is to prescribe mind-altering drugs–for which they do not always provide sufficient monitoring and follow-up. It has often been pointed out that American women take inordinate amounts of sleeping pills, energizers, tranquilizers, and other medication. *Behavior Today* reported on May 1, 1978:

> According to the National Institute on Drug Abuse, women receive almost twice as many prescriptions for psychoactive drugs as men, and female admissions to emergency rooms for treatment of drug-related disorders are currently running at almost twice the male rate. NIDA estimates that 2 million American women are now dependent on prescription drugs, and that many members of this group overlap with the 5 million estimated to be alcoholics, despite the fact that the combination of liquor and drugs is dangerous and sometimes fatal.

Iatrogenic disease–disease caused by physicians–is common among older women. However, not all adverse reactions to medication are the fault of physicians. Doctorers themselves cause some, usually inspired by advertisements that promise relief and happiness. Older women buy massive quantities of over-the-counter nonprescription remedies. If physicians asked their patients to bring in a shopping bag of all the medications they take, they might be shocked to discover very large collections, including medicines that duplicate one another's action and react together poorly.

Lack of compliance with physician's advice is one of the biggest problems in American medicine. Many people do not complete a course of treatment once they begin to feel better. But doctorers overcomply. They may continue refilling and taking prescriptions long after the doctor intended, thus creating iatrogenic disease and drug dependence.

Special Medical Problems

Many feminists have criticized physicians for performing excessive surgery on women, including radical mastectomies when less drastic surgery would be sufficient. Hysterectomies are more common in the United States than in any other country. Some feminists claim that many of these operations result from a surplus of surgeons in certain geographic areas. "Important changes in sexuality" follow hysterectomy according to one researcher, Dr. Suzanne Morgan, writing in the January/February 1978 *Women & Health*. Many older women who have had the operation, wonder if it was necessary. Some are necessary, of course, but not all that are done. Mabel tells this story, which is repeated by other interviewees:

I went to the gynecologist for my annual checkup, and he said I had a large fibroid uterine tumor and had better have a hysterectomy immediately because such tumors can become cancerous. Later I found out this is highly unlikely, but I'd already had the operation. I didn't want the operation so he sent me to another gynecologist for a second opinion. This man said his colleague was right. So I had the operation because I was scared of cancer. When I came out of anesthesia, Dr. Brown told me that while operating he had also removed my ovaries and appendix. I asked him if there was anything wrong with either and he said no, but he took them out so nothing would happen in the future. I was annoyed, but he couldn't very well put them back. My tumor was not malignant, the lab said. My son in medical school told me they have now discovered that the appendix does have some antibacterial and other

*functions. Also, because my ovaries were both removed, I had no
natural estrogen and the doctor put me on estrogen pills. Then
there was the scare about estrogen causing cancer and this made
me worry, so I quit. I really don't know why he had to clean me out
like a chicken. I also have heard many fibroids shrink as you get
older so I wonder if the operation was really necessary.*

Actually Mabel, who lost several organs, was not a true doc-
torer. She was simply scared and obedient. True doctorers seek
medical intervention to change their lives; some magnify every
discomfort into a threat and thus are liable to be drugged or subjected to surgical or other drastic procedures.

Not all doctorers can afford good care. It is estimated that up
to 17 percent of older women cannot afford medical care at all,
and facilities for the poor are frequently not inviting or conven-
ient and seem designed to give medical students experience
rather than to help patients. However, this chapter is not about
American medicine, unequalitarian though it is. It is about the
women who make a way of life out of their real or imagined
illnesses.

Some of the depressed or anxious older women who have
funds or appropriate insurance benefits go to or are referred to
psychiatrists, psychologists, social workers, and other
psychotherapists—with or without credentials. Some get help,
some are harmed (as discussed earlier) and still others pass time
this way and make a career out of patienthood. As one perpetual
psychiatric patient said: "It is the 'golden hour' when someone
listens." The paid friendship fills a void.

Often badly in need of doctoring are single women whose relationships with men have broken up. An unmarried woman who
has lived with a man for many years may suffer just as deeply
when the relationship ends as a married woman. Nonetheless,
she seldom receives the comfort and support extended to the
widow or even the limited amount of sympathy extended a di-

vorced woman. It is particularly humiliating to a single woman when her man abandons her for someone younger after a long affair. As a liberated woman, she does not insist on marriage or a permanent commitment, and she has no protection. She feels rejected and a fool at the same time. Besides, she may have no furniture and no energy to establish a new home. There are women who have, regretfully, had abortions because men were not yet ready to marry, only to lose them a few years later to someone else, usually younger. It is no wonder that such women, deeply wounded and angry, sometimes develop psychosomatic illnesses for they may have permanently lost their opportunity for motherhood.

Changing sexual patterns have created considerable conflict for women of all ages, and stress often leads to illness. The protection of sorts afforded by the old rules is gone, and in many sexual relationships ethics are gone too. New sorts of exploitation appear in supposedly equal relationships. Single women put lovers through school just as wives do, and they often get heartache and rejection when they are past the easily marriageable age.

Single women and married ones also get venereal disease and suffer terrible discomfort and feelings of self-repugnance. As ethical beings many of them give up sexual activity so as not to infect lovers – a courtesy that is less often extended by men.

Being Alone – A Medical Problem?

One reason some older women seek help from therapists and the medical profession is that they often lack the aid and reassurance provided by others who care or who have experienced similar pains and crises. Geographic distance and class mobility have dispersed many families; and many older women live especially isolated, lonely lives. One country woman of 40 had to go to a terrible nursing home when she had a bad case of the flu because there was no one to bring her groceries or supplies at home. Usually

though, loners are clustered in urban areas, where transportation, jobs, and apartments are plentiful but community and close
neighboring or social resources are scarce.

One older woman who applied for an apartment in a housing
project had no relative to list on the form requesting a name in
case of emergency. Her situation was not unusual. She wrote instead the name of the nurse at a clinic; the nurse at least knew
her and could be trusted. Links with medical people are sometimes all older women have.

Properly distrustful in urban settings or isolated in rural
ones, there are only a few places older women can take their anxiety. Priscilla, a widow of 60, explained: "Once in a while I wake
up at night terrified. I am frightened to be alone but where can
you go at 3:00 A.M.? I don't drink, so I couldn't go to a bar, even if
one were still open. If things really get bad, hospitals are one
place that run 24 hours a day. It's nice to know you can always go
to the emergency room, and I have a couple times when I was in
panic and my heart pounded. They don't do anything much, but
there are people there. They check me out and let me stay until I
feel in control. I know they think I'm a fake but really I feel so
awful sometimes."

Even if she was thought a nuisance by the hospital staff,
Priscilla needed this safety valve to survive her terror. With her
limited options, her seemingly demanding behavior was healthier
and less self-destructive than some of the people to be described in
the next chapter—the escapists and isolates.

The tragedy is that doctorers desperately conjure up physical
symptoms to get attention or company they have almost no other
way of getting. They are criticized for using medical facilities un-
necessarily, but few attempts are made to meet their real needs.
For example, a municipal public health service stopped offering
once-a-week free blood pressure checks because a sizable number
of older women came every single time, even though the administrator thought their visits unnecessary. The women found it
something to do of an empty afternoon, and they liked the atten-

tion and reassurance given them by the nurse and chatting with other women waiting their turn. The authorities, in cutting off this medical service, never considered what substitute program of a nonmedical nature might be offered to these obviously needy women. A coffee hour or the chance to do something useful or meaningful would almost certainly have been welcomed. Instead, the women got a closed door and a bad reputation. For the over-60 there are many facilities, but there are practically none for younger older women.

Cult Healing

It is no surprise that some older women, discouraged by the certified professional, turn to the uncertified. They move from healer to healer, seeking magic to restore vitality, beauty, youth, and social value. Their hopes are often high, if unrealistic, but they will settle for a sympathetic ear. In recent years some have turned to women's organizations for good or bad advice and treatment.

Healing cults have become institutionalized in some parts of the women's movement as attempts to replace lost neighborhood mutual aid. Uncredentialed healers abound among militant women who reject the medical model or have been rejected by doctors. Distressed older women respond to such ads as the following, which was distributed and posted widely in one metropolis:

SELF-HEALING

an opportunity to use six LOVE PROJECT principles to unravel the complicated energy web of spiritual, mental, emotional and physical disease and illness. Applying this LOVE PROJECT "healing kit," we will see clearly what we did to create the condition we now have, positive or negative, and will begin awakening the Self to its inner harmony and rhythm. A day-long session, from 10 A.M. to 10 P.M. to provide extensive exploration of LOVE PROJECT principles and practice in using them to create a new and healthful way of life. Maximum 50 people.

One interesting example of the new healers is Womoncraft, a self-help course taught by women using a manual composed by other noncredentialed women. It employs many techniques from meditation and various avant-garde therapies. Largely by word of mouth and through women's organizations, this course and others like it have spread rapidly throughout the country. Thousands of women have become involved in Womoncraft. The course is offered to women at a small token fee and supposedly trains them to heal themselves and others and "to develop their psychic powers." As one student of social movements, Hans Toch, has said: "The winter of discontent evokes the summer of faith." He points out, in *The Social Psychology of Social Movements* (p. 16), that "for a person to be led to join a social movement, he must not only sense a problem but also (1) feel that something can be done about it and (2) want to do something about it." This is precisely the situation experienced by many doctorers. In Toch's view, society creates a problem situation, and the impact of the situation creates a problem for individuals, some of whom are susceptible to the appeals of social movements. The result is what John Wilson calls "the mobilization of discontent." Hurt and hoping women join.

I did a participant-observer study of Womoncraft, attending the course and the spring equinox celebration of what was called "the life force perpetuating and rejuvenating all in nature." Many other older women were in the course, though presumably I was the only sociologist doing research.

The bible for some Womoncraft healers is Hungarian-born Z. Budapest's *The Feminist Book of Light and Shadows*. In it Budapest is described as "the high Priestess of her coven," which worships the Goddess Diana. She suggests that "when somebody is ill and all herbal medicines and doctor's medicines don't help, lay the naked person in a beam of full moonlight. Take a basket of 13 fresh eggs, rub one at a time on the person's skin slowly touching all crevices, saying, "by the power of Diana, by the power of

Aradia, may all that is ill be absorbed into this egg. . . . etc." (p. 86). Presumably this technique works as well as other cures for certain psychosomatic illnesses.

Most Womoncraft lore is less exotic, emphasizing massage, guided fantasies, and affirmations such as "I am healthy and strong." Certainly, lonely older women find warmth and acceptance from Womoncraft healers. Even some educated women with responsible professional jobs in corporations are taking Womoncraft seriously. By the time this is published, however, there will probably be a newer women's health fad.

It is interesting that self-help groups of many sorts seem to be welcomed by some certain medical professionals, who are referring more and more of what they call their "crocks" to them. For example, several years ago the Massachusetts division of Blue Cross distributed, without approving, a booklet listing self-help groups; some, in my opinion, were of dubious value. But if older women and others are channeled into such groups, instead of to physicians and hospitals, it will cut down on the third-party payments for medical services. They may also relieve doctors who cannot help stigmatized and rejected persons—usually the poor. Many such groups, such as Alcoholics Anonymous, have a good success rate, but others are poor and especially harmful if a person uses them for a condition that requires scientific medicine.

Of course, women are not the only ones involved in self-help groups or in promoting strange health ways. Not long ago, a speaker from a federal agency, himself a physician, performed a guided fantasy for a Washington, D.C., audience of college graduates and middle-aged persons, mostly women. I will condense what took about twenty minutes with the lights out and soft music playing. He said: "Imagine going deep into yourself and finding there a door into a little room. You furnish this little room with things you like. In the room is a little doctor. You like him and you tell him what is bothering you, and you feel better. Now that you know where he is and how to get to him, you can go there anytime you need help." His audience seemed to go along with his fantasy. And, if they seek out the little doctor or Womoncraft, there will be no medical charges.

Certainly in this society some people need to be more self-reliant. On the other hand, the most gullible people of all are probably those whose internal little doctor might be prone to misdiagnose and mistreat. For a government physician to put his stamp of approval on such matters is not as bizarre as it may seem; the government, like insurers, is worried about mounting medical costs, and its concerns are justified by mounting taxes and taxpayers' revolts. Still there must be better solutions than encouraging people to lose touch with reality.

Society and Medical Costs

Some national leaders feel that undue expectations for health care have been raised and that people should be guided to expect less. When allocations of scarce resources are made, it is inevitable that those with the least power and money will be diverted from services or given the least. Soon society will have to make hard decisions about mounting medical costs, for under the present system the costs will soar over the next decades as a higher percentage of us become old. According to *Facts About Older Americans* (HEW), 10.9 percent of us, 23 million people, are now over 65; but by the year 2000 the figure will go up to 12.2 percent—nearly 32 million people. In 1976 the nation spent approximately $120 billion for personal health care; about 29 percent of this was for older persons. As the implications of these figures have begun to be understood, the backlash has set in.

People who are not yet 65, including many women in their forties, fifties, and sixties, are being told not to look to the medical establishment for so much help. Yet there is no concerted attempt to determine what could be done to make their lives and society happier and healthier.

Some doctorers are denied the real medical help they need, while others seek inappropriate remedies for what are poor options rather than medical conditions. Both kinds of doctorers are victims of the neglect of older women, which has high costs for themselves and society.

Medication turns some women into escapists, and rejections by medical personnel and other people turns others into isolates. Older women who are escapists and isolates are discussed in the next chapter.

CHAPTER NINE

Escapists and Isolates

AT 45 FRANCINE has become both an isolate and escapist. She tells the following story:

After I got my divorce, I lived alone for the first time in my life. My children are on their own—in fact, I waited to end a terrible marriage until they were grown. The kind of assembly work I do is lonely. My friends are still married, and I rarely see them now. I find myself spending a lot of time wandering around stores in my time off because, well, it is someplace to be where there are people. I also find myself angry a lot of the time, but I don't know how to get rid of the feeling.

What has happened is that I have begun to steal. I take little things from stores and public places—things I don't really need and could probably afford to buy. I'm not sure why I take them. Maybe it's kind of getting back at the world. I think I want something and I can't get it. But I'm afraid I'll get caught. Maybe I want to. At least someone will know I exist.

Francine may indeed be noticed. Except for being ridiculed or scorned, escapists and isolates usually get attention only when they are blatantly deviant or overt tragedy calls attention to them.

Though Francine's kleptomania was an escape from her isolation, not all escapists are isolates. Many have kin or friends, but their relationships with them are not good or sustaining for a variety of reasons. Indeed, some escapists are running from too many demands and burdens rather than from loneliness. And, though some isolates turn into escapists of various sorts, not all do. Some suffer on as isolates, adjusting to their aloneness and managing somehow.

Both isolates and escapists can turn into doctorers because their habits can and do undermine their mental and physical health. Certainly doctorers can also be escapists or isolates.

It is worth remembering at this point that persons can play out more than one role at a time; the roles have been more or less artificially separated in these chapters for analytical purposes. Any particular individual may have a wide repertoire; we have role bundles not single roles, though at any given time one or more roles may be paramount.

In the situation of deprived older women, escapism and isolation are often linked; isolates frequently become escapists. They find relief where they can. Conversely, deteriorated escapists often isolate themselves or are rejected and isolated by others. It is a vicious circle in which many older women spin.

Suicide

Their spinning takes many forms—drug dependence, alcoholism, frenetic searches for diversion, overeating, lethargy and the ultimate escape: suicide. Suicide, which has been more common among older men who are alone, is beginning to rise among older women too. Publicized suicides by famous mid-life women have provided disastrous role models for women losing hope and meaning as they age. Imitation follows desperation: "If, with all her talent and beauty, she couldn't go on, why should I?" depressives think.

It is difficult to assess the number of female suicides after 35 because the statistics are unreliable. Suicides are frequently covered up by families and physicians because of the stigma. But the number is generally believed to be substantial and growing.

Suicide can represent anger at a particular person or the world, or it can indicate the endpoint of isolation and the lack of hope for integration. All human roles are reciprocal, and each player has a role partner or partners with whom the drama of social interaction is played out. A teacher cannot teach without students, a parent must have a child, and a lover a loved one. Even the seemingly alone isolate has a partner of sorts. The partner is perhaps only imaginary—a fantasized lover or friend—or it may be the community itself. The loner hopes a partner will notice, care, and rescue. Many suicide attempts are such calls for help.

Movie and television personalities or figures from their pasts float through the fantasies of many isolated persons, including some older women. Fantasies can sustain some people indefinitely, but others are not satisfied by such remote role partners. When hope no longer exists for ways to play the real drama of life, they withdraw from it. Older, separated women or divorcées are a group especially at risk for suicide. Many feel that their lives are over, and they hasten to bring down the curtain. This is especially true if they feel they have been betrayed by a spouse.

Alcoholism

It is also difficult to estimate the number of older female alcoholics, although authorities believe their ranks are substantial and growing. The December 1977 *Statistical Bulletin* of the Metropolitan Life Insurance Company reported that between 1963 and 1964 and 1973 and 1974, mortality from alcoholic disorders increased 36 percent for white females 20 years and over and 71 percent for minority females over 20. The highest increases, however, were in the older ages; 23 percent for white women between ages 40 and 49 and 91 percent for nonwhite women in the same age group; 46 percent for white women aged 50 to 59 and 122 percent for nonwhites. At ages 60 to 69, the increase was 73 percent for white women and 121 percent for minority women. The bulletin added: "the true impact of the disease is hard to measure, however, because of considerable underreporting of alcoholism as a cause of death" (p. 5).

The differential between nonwhite and white women may represent more than the fact that life is harder for minority older women. Nonwhites are more apt to be poor and to die in public facilities, so their deaths are more frequently reported as due to alcoholism. Wealthier women's private doctors may put a different cause of death on the certificate to spare the family and the deceased's reputation. There is considerable drinking in country clubs and fashionable condominiums and behind sedate suburban evergreens as middle- or upper-class ladies drink quietly alone or with other bored or unhappy women. Alcohol brings companions or substitutes for them. It also drowns, at least temporarily, sadness about feeling useless, wrinkled, and unwanted. Women who are abused by their husbands often seek solace by drinking alone–ashamed to share their grief with family or friends.

Occupants of single rooms in inner-city, rundown hotels or boardinghouses or of unattractive tiny apartments, can and do form drinking cliques. Such women seek both relief from a painfully difficult environment and some kind of human contact. Bars, can be substitute homes at all hours. Many people without families have "their bar" where they experience a kind of pseudo intimacy by being recognized by employees and other customers.

Living Alone

Though some older women alone are beginning to experiment with communal living, many still have very lonely residence arrangements. According to the Women's Bureau of the U.S. Department of Labor, nearly 6.4 million white women and 660,000 minority women 55 years of age and over were not living in families in 1974. These 7 million women accounted for 31 percent of all women aged 55 and over. Among women aged 14 and over who were not living in families, more than six out of ten were 55 or older. In addition, 93 percent of white women over 45 not living in families were living alone; and 87 percent of minority women not in families were alone. There are also many women younger than 45 who live alone or with children who do not provide much companionship. With the current trend of very small families, most women are through childrearing at quite early ages; and many women do not marry at all or lose their husbands to death or divorce by mid-life.

Sociologists have long known that lack of social integration is pathogenic—that is, it predisposes people to depression and suicide. Men and women living alone need outside contacts in order to be integrated into social institutions. But many older women do not have those contacts, as previous chapters have shown. Predominating in the older age groups, women alone rank disproportionately high among the nation's isolates. Mental hospital admission rates are high for such women.

Socialized to nurture others, women often feel lost when they are on their own. When it becomes apparent they will not marry, some women adopt children or have fantasies of doing so. They cannot conceive of a meaningful life without sharing.

Certainly there are some people who enjoy living alone and are happy in solitary pursuits. But most human beings require human contact and caring. Early in the development of social science, it was learned that isolated children failed to grow normally and actually gave up and died for lack of love and human contact. During World War II, English babies removed from their families in the cities as protection from air raids sickened even though they were well cared for physically. These babies had multiple caretakers but little personal attention and affection. When caretakers were assigned individual babies and told to give them love, the infants improved dramatically.

In the same way, some older women alone have felt so estranged from life that they did not change their clothes for weeks, even slept in them. Life became a torpor of bare existence. Despair was covered up by lethargy. They existed on toast and tea or junk food. Yet, when these women were brought into a sheltered workshop with caring others, they changed quite dramatically. They bathed, took care of themselves, ate properly, responded to people, and reached out to them. They were glad to be alive and almost embarrassingly grateful for the help that made this possible. However, rescuing older women is not a high community priority. Most women have to work at maintaining contacts. And they work against great handicaps.

Isolation is not chosen, but it becomes the debilitating condition of poorly paid or unemployed never-married people or those who were once married, including many minority women living in unsafe neighborhoods with poor or hazardous public transportation. The cab drivers who reject older female fares generally dislike most of all driving older women at night into deteriorated urban neighborhoods. Since economic necessity forces such housing on many women, they do not dare to go out at night. In any case many do not have recreational funds.

During childhood, girls more than boys are taught to value close relationships with others. When women lack these later in life and experience rejection, they begin to pity and even despise themselves. If others do not consider them worthy of attention, they sometimes stop caring about or attending to themselves. They neglect their health and appearance and are thought peculiar—and are even more disdained.

Often in their younger years these women were busy wives and mothers who never developed close relationships outside the home. Responsibilities, and sometimes the husband's jealousy, or the couples' closeness prevented other involvements. Alone for the first time in their lives and less resilient than young people, such women often report anxiety attacks. Sometimes in quiet rooms or even on busy streets they lose control and call out the names of lost spouses or of children now grown and gone. They become upset when they do this, especially in public, because they know they are fantasizing. They cry out their losses despite themselves.

Many say they often feel like crying but run from tears because they are afraid that if they start they will never be able to stop. What they mean is that there will be no one to comfort them or to help them, and they must maintain control at all costs. Maintaining such tight control over the emotions creates such unconscious explosion that in the end eruption ensues. Often the eruption comes in the form of hostile behavior over quite minor slights. Unable to attack the real sources of their pain, they turn upon whatever targets are available. Since older women often receive insults, targets are not hard to find.

One usually reserved and dignified new divorcée was embarrassed after she made a scene because the waitress first served several couples who came in after she did. The waitress's neglect triggered her deep anger about more serious deprivations. She had no companions with whom to have dinner. She was one of the women who had had to hold a job and be a homemaker too and had not had the luxury of developing social networks or hobbies. When their children are grown, many of these women do not know how to meet their needs for interaction.

The Dispossessed

Almost every city has a deteriorating area in which older women live in pitiful furnished rooms or on the street. Very early in the morning, the most dispossessed may be seen scavenging through barrels, seeking something to use or sell. Many are ill, malnourished, and chronically desperate. These "bag ladies" or homeless women are not counted in official statistics, but almost every urban area has its share. Their population has been swelled in recent years by the emptying of mental hospitals—overtly out of humanitarian motives. One cannot help wondering, however, how much the move to de-institutionalization is financially motivated, for little or no consistent follow-up care is provided for discharges.

Among the poor and needy older women are many who, having lost their breadwinners and untrained for any job, do not know how to fit into the economy. They have no funding and few social supports; and, as we have seen in preceding chapters, they are often rejected in their efforts to find roles. Discouragement can and often does lead to withdrawal from the mainstream and to deviant roles as all others are closed.

Mary, whose unemployed husband disappeared when the two children were babies, is an example. Although a bright woman, Mary came from a poor rural family and only completed eighth grade. To support her children, she took care of other people's children, leaving her own untended. She was too proud to take what she called "charity" and also feared that if she did the social workers would take away her children. No one ever told Mary she was entitled, for example, to an education.

At 16 years old Mary's son was shot and killed in a burglary; he had tried unsuccessfully to get work. Then, to start a new life, Mary's 18-year-old daughter moved across the country and discouraged Mary from following her. Grieving for her son and ashamed about his death, Mary could not face living alone in her unsafe area. So she sold her furniture for a few dollars and took a live-in maid's job. Though her wages were low, she felt a part of her employer's family for fifteen years and loved the children. However, when the children went off to college, Mary was no longer needed.

At 51, she looked much older; she had lost her teeth and had no dentures. She soon exhausted her small savings and could not find another job. Her employer had not paid social security for her. Mary did not ask her daughter for help; by this time she had children of her own. Eventually and with great difficulty, Mary obtained a small amount of aid but it was not really enough to live on. When she got her monthly pittance, she would move into a cheap room; when the money ran out, she would find shelter in libraries, train stations, bus depots and wherever she could, carrying her possessions in a bag and singing hymns aloud to sustain herself. People on the streets thought her crazy. And indeed, since she had nobody else to talk to, she talked aloud to herself as she walked. She was often hungry. Loneliness drove her to visit her old employers a few times, but she did not feel welcome and stopped going. Though she did not drink, she sometimes pretended to be an alcoholic so she could sleep in a shelter for such women. At least there was food and company there. But mostly, Mary was completely alone. She often thought of killing herself but was afraid of "eternal hell."

Not all isolates or escapists are economically as distressed or as unknowledgeable as Mary. Some even have education and money; but, because they are surplus as older women, they lack companionship and meaning in their lives. Alone most of the time, they find themselves talking to themselves, and this distresses them. They worry about "going crazy." Indeed, they are sometimes described as "loony" by others if, in their loneliness, they develop peculiarities. Many keep the television or radio on all the time for company or have pets to talk to and love. Six or seven cats can provide a family of sorts. One never-married woman accumulated four dogs by the age of 40. They were company, she said. Others have more dangerous coping mechanisms or compensations.

Sarah Montgomery was one such older women. A debutante in 1940, she was a graduate of a liberal arts college but did not seek paid work because in the 1940s wealthy young women were expected to stay home, help at charitable events, and prepare for good marriages. In 1941 she did marry a young man; a few years later he was killed in World War II. No children were born of the brief union. During the war and for a few years afterward Sarah did Red Cross volunteer work. She lived comfortably on income from her husband's military insurance and money given her by his parents and her family. She would have liked to remarry and have children, but the opportunity never presented itself. Now and then she thought she should train for a job; but she didn't know what kind, and her relatives discouraged her. Her father said: "Why take a job away from some family man." Anyway she was kept busy being a companion to her parents and in-laws. Driving them about and doing errands and such filled her days; she felt needed and useful.

However, by the time Sarah reached 55, she had nursed the last of the four parents through a final illness. She suddenly found herself quite alone and terribly bored and anxious. Her income now, because of inflation, did not go far, and she couldn't afford luxuries like travel. She tried to keep busy by breeding dogs and raising flowers but she grew increasingly lonely. She was glad when the phone rang, even if it was only a salesman. Many weeks it never rang at all. Because the neighborhood around it had changed, the church she had always attended was closed. Eventually, she had to leave herself because the neighborhood was no longer safe. She resisted moving until she was hit in the back of the head with a brick and robbed. She knew some elderly people who boarded themselves into their old home and lived like prisoners, relying on delivery men for supplies. She did not want to become like them. So, with great difficulty, she moved to a suburb.

There she found herself surrounded by young families who offered brief "hellos" when they saw her outdoors. But they never came to her house and never invited her to theirs. The sounds of the families saddened her because she felt so alone.

She asked the local hospital if she could do volunteer work but they had a long waiting list. She answered an ad for a job but was not even interviewed. She went to the church of her denomination, but, though the people nodded politely, nobody seemed interested in getting to know her. After a while, she stopped going She gardened and cleaned her house, but she found herself crying a great deal. Her old family doctor had died, and when she told her new young doctor she was depressed, he said: "It's just your nerves. You are really a fortunate woman. Stop feeling sorry for yourself." She felt ashamed and rebuffed.

Her family had always served champagne or wine on festive occasions, but Sarah had never drunk alone. Her appetite was poor, and to build herself up she began to make milkshakes with a generous amount of vanilla extract (35 percent alcohol). Gradually she added more and more extract. Soon, she stopped adding the milk. She had become an alcoholic, although she denied this to herself.

Since she had no close friends or family, her drinking went unnoticed for years. Finally, she broke her leg falling down the stairs when intoxicated. She was discovered after her neighbors heard her dog barking for two days. She was hospitalized, and her addiction and deterioration were discovered. A distant relative took over her financial affairs, and Sarah was institutionalized. She never returned home and died in the institution at less than 60 years old, a victim of social isolation.

It is always easy to blame the victim. Some neighbors said Sarah should have found something to do with her life, but they had never made any suggestions. Nobody had ever asked her to babysit, for example. She had been brought up during an era when girls of her class were not prepared for any role other than wifehood and motherhood. When she lost the chance to play these roles, nobody helped her to find a new one. As she aged, she lost her relatives and her neighborhood, a common fate in these days of rapid social change and geographic mobility. Few people reach out to women like this to prepare them for their older years or help them when they reach them. There are extensive services for those over 65 and for youth. The late middle-aged and early-old fall by the wayside. Actually Sarah could have been trained for many useful years of work or activities; and she would thus have been integrated into new networks. But she couldn't do this alone, and nobody was watching. Nobody cared. So, like many isolates, she deteriorated and tried to escape her pain, with sad consequences.

Older women in similar situations turn to food, rather than alcohol for escape or comfort. It may be the only gratification available to women with limited resources. But they do not eat entirely out of pleasure. Many report they don't even taste the food, rather chewing is a way of expressing anger or other emotions. In supermarkets such women eat candy or cookies from ripped-open packages, sometimes they throw away the empty wrapper even before reaching the checkout counter. It is one way of grabbing something. Before you feel disgusted, think about what else is or is not available to these women. Isolates escape from loneliness by buying time and space with people in stores and in restaurants. Going out to eat is a substitute for human relationships and denied activities.

Escapists who turn to food may be found in the clothing shops that cater to the obese. Such stores are characterized by the desperation with which customers hunt through racks or bins, hoping for an item of clothing that will make them look acceptable. In addition to the prejudice experienced as an aging female, obese women encounter widespread discrimination. It is noteworthy that the employees in many of these stores, though not always obese, are generally less attractive than those in other shops. Do they find a home with other dispossessed women, or are these low-status stores the only ones that will hire them?

Many minority women are overweight because of starchy low-income diets or because life offers them little else than food. Moreover, companionship is frequently organized around eating.

Some obese escapists are also seekers and make the circuit of diet clubs, although they seldom lose weight (they usually put it back on if they do). Like the "fat lady store" the clubs are someplace to go; they are one place the obese belong and are accepted. They are better than the isolation that otherwise pervades their lives. In fact, these women have an investment in remaining compulsive eaters—at least it provides them with an identity and gives them importance of a sort. They are noticed in a world that ignores older women.

Finding Companionship—Problems and Some Solutions

Of course, not all older women alone turn to drink or food. Some make heroic efforts to keep occupied and integrated. Mrs. Lewis, a widow, explains what she does:

I like to know my neighbors. I call on all new neighbors. I volunteer to collect every year for the community chest and also for a couple of other drives. That way I get to meet people and remind them I'm around. Also, I do errands for shut-ins. I feel like I'm doing something. However, with the inflation and all, I think I won't collect anymore because lately, I notice people don't give and then they avoid me.

I really look forward to Halloween, when the little kids come to the door. It is really lonely living in this town. It has no public transportation. I tried a million times to get a job but I couldn't. I'm lucky I have enough to live on, but I wish I had enough to make more long distance calls. My kids live away, and I only see them a few times a year. That is not much to make a life on.

You just can't clean house or watch TV all day. You can take just so many walks and all that, especially in the winter. One thing that helps is that a month ago they started a swimnastics class in the indoor pool at the "Y." There are a dozen women in the class, and it is fun to do the exercises together. I am going to try to find out if any of the others live alone, and maybe I could invite them back here for a cup of coffee some time.

Unlike Sarah Montgomery, Mrs. Lewis is still reaching out to survive as an older woman alone. She is not as angry as women like Miss T., who lives on the next street. Mrs. Lewis does not know her because, except for the new swimnastics class, there are few places in their community where mid-life loners can meet.

One day, Miss T., who lost her job recently, took all the antidepressant pills her doctor had given her. She felt life was not worth living. After overdosing, she did call the police, so her suicide was aborted. However, her cry for help was answered by a stomach pump, a few kind words from her doctor, and a stern warning. She really needs more. Unless her life has some human contact, Miss T. may not call the police next time. Many do not, or they call too late and the cry for help becomes a completed suicide.

Miss T. tells her story:

I had a very demanding executive secretarial job and was very proud to do it well. I always got there before my boss, though he was in early, and I always stayed late after he left to make sure everything was cleaned up. But when the company promoted and moved him, they did not move me. They asked me to take early retirement, although I was only 55. I didn't want to, and I felt terrible that nobody in the company could find a place for me after all the years I gave them. I needed weekends for errands and house-cleaning when I was workng and never developed hobbies. My friends were at work. I lost them when I lost the job.

When I asked Miss T. why she didn't sue for discrimination on age, which is illegal, she replied: "Oh I couldn't do that, I wouldn't know how. Besides, I'd be too ashamed to make an uproar. Maybe I was slowing down. I can see the men wanted attractive secretaries. Besides, I understand you have to have a lawyer, and I didn't want to spend any of my money because I felt I would lose anyway and I should save my money to live on."

Afraid to take a risk, Miss T. would also never consider taking desperate measures to find companionship. Other older women are less afraid or more hopeful. To read personal ads is to see their hopes, usually futile.

The following ads are from a syndicated column called "Dates Galore" that appears weekly in a number of giveaway television schedule "ad" magazines. They were all selected from one issue of a suburban edition, but they are typical of ads appearing in newspapers and magazines throughout the country.

Attractive middle-aged woman, free of responsibilities, would like to meet someone who is kind, considerate, enjoys life, good companionship. Nothing is enjoyable without someone to share it with. Will answer all sincere replies.

I am 40 looking for someone who is as lonely as I am. I want someone for companionship. Someone that will treat a lady like she should be treated.

Widow, 65, 5'8" light brown hair, brown eyes, 180 lbs. I am very lonesome and like to go out to eat, movies, rides, some TV, read and love to cook.

Attractive, white widow, 65 5'5½", 165 lbs. I enjoy movies, dancing, dining out, travel. Would like to meet a nice interesting man for companionship about my age.

The last ad notes "would like to meet a . . . man . . . about my age." Most women, however, listed no age for men or suggested ranges considerably older than their own, knowing that this is the way the dating-mating game works. This age disparity is clearly demonstrated by the male ads in the same week's column. Not only were there far fewer older men looking for women, most of the men's ads specified, as usual, younger women.

41, 5'8" 160 lbs., good looking. Would like to meet a loving, affectionate, good looking woman early to mid 30's. Photo if possible.

Hello! I'm 56 & looking for a nice girl that don't drink or smoke & is not a nervous wreck about 38-50, 5'5"-5'8". There is a lot of things I would like to do also, so let me hear from you.

I am 50, 5'11", 175 lbs., gray hair, blue eyes. Would like correspondence with slim home-type woman under 40. Send photo & interests, hobbies, etc.

There are some exceptions to men's preference for younger women. A few older women report themselves besieged by much younger men, and some have liaisons with them. Others say, "it doesn't feel right to me," or "they seem like babies," or "who needs to be his mother?" But in general older women have few sexual opportunities. In fact, many greeted with indignation the 1978 film *An Unmarried Woman* because the newly divorced heroine was pictured as young and besieged by lovers, even though she had a 15-year-old daughter and had been married a long time. Most women felt the picture was totally unreflective of their isolation.

Though most older women feel uncomfortable at singles' bars and clubs, one grateful woman who discovered a New England group called The Single Life—which sponsors weekly discussions and social events—wrote the following letter to the *T.S.L. Newsletter*.

Let me tell you about my impression of TSL!

I lost seven years of my life because I did not know about it earlier!! Seven lonely years! Tearsome, fearsome, awful, desperately lonely years . . . Not even an ad in the Want Advertiser would help. Until TSL changed my life. It helped me to recognize that I was not the only lonely person on earth. It gave me new friends, of both sexes. It made it possible for me to take part in many lovely entertainments, from nature walks to theater-experiences or dances. Finally I even met "my dream man"!

Seven years, when you are not a spring chick anyway, is too long a time!!

Such organizations are relatively rare, though there are many persons willing to make money exploiting older women and many commercial dating services. Some religious organizations are realizing the isolation of single persons. The Unitarian-Universalist Association, for example, has established a new position for a director of single-life programs.

Not all denominations are so alert to the problem of those alone, however. Recently, I was shocked to see in a newspaper ad for a large religious congregation holding an open house to recruit congregants, the words "Families Invited." I wrote to the clergyman, pointing out that many people today are not imbedded in families and suggesting that just possibly they were the people who most needed welcoming. I also pointed out that because the median age of the population is increasing, it is in the self-interest of religious organizations to get away from "pediatric religion," in which activities revolve around childrens' needs. He wrote back a very defensive and to me offensive letter in which he said that the word "families" was inadvertent and that I had over-reacted. Still, the next week the ad was changed to "People Invited," so I felt my consciousness-raising was worthwhile. Actually it is precisely such unawareness of existence of people who are alone that is so damaging to them.

In 1978 I held a workshop for clergymen and lay religious leaders from throughout the country. Some interesting data emerged when I asked them to write, anonymously on index cards, the answers to two questions: (1) How are older women's needs met in your congregation? (2) How are older women used as a resource in your congregation? The answers to question 1 were long lists of neglect. Answers to question 2 were sparse.

If your community is doing little to help isolates, it is typical. Most activities are oriented toward families. Isolates are sometimes made lonelier by being in situations that remind them of their aloneness. The world seems set up for couples.

One woman, recovering from the trauma of her divorce, decided to treat herself to a subscription series of theater tickets. Her married friends were not available to go with her, and she had not made any new close friends. Imagine her surprise when, after sending her check for one subscription to the series, she received two tickets for each show. The clerk stuffing the envelopes had, like most other people, the Noah's Ark syndrome.

Certainly many older women come to terms with celibacy and living alone, and they find satisfactory ways to manage the situation. What is extraordinary is the strength and many excellent survivorship skills developed by isolated and deprived women. Eleanor, for example, is a well-educated woman of 58 whose last steady full-time job ended several years ago when the social agency she worked for lost its funding. After her unemployment compensation ran out, she had to settle for a part-time cashier's job in a cafeteria. She barely manages to pay for her room and food on her pay. Except at work, she is alone almost all the time. However, she has learned to use a food co-op, free health clinics, and other community resources. She swims at public pools during the summer. In the winter she walks in the back door of an exclusive hotel, leaves her coat on the rack outside the restaurant, and goes to swim in the indoor pool and use the sauna for free, using the ladies room to get out of her wet suit. She looks the part of a prosperous hotel guest because she buys her clothes at a hospital thrift shop supplied by wealthy physicians' wives.

Though she lives in a one-room apartment, she gardens in the summer and has fresh vegetables for her table. This is because she signed up early for a plot in the city's public gardens. She goes to free movies at the library and keeps an ear cocked for other free events. One of the places on her itinerary is the local art gallery; once a month the gallery has a Sunday opening where wine, sandwiches, and pastries are served. The people at the gallery are annoyed because Eleanor consumes a great many sandwiches and several glasses of wine and pastries, but they do not want to make a scene—something Eleanor banks on. Actually, Eleanor enjoys the exhibitions and being with the people as much as the refreshments. When she is at the pool or in the art gallery, however, Eleanor sometimes has her pleasure spoiled by the fact that everyone else seems to be with someone. Once, after she had taken a great deal of trouble to sneak into a pool, she left because an older couple in the pool were being very attentive to each other. Suddenly, she felt lonelier than ever.

Eleanor worries about what will happen when she gets older. When she gets older she may or may not become like Jacquelyn. Jacquelyn also swims a lot, not so much because she likes swimming, as because there are no bathing facilities in her apartment—an illegal attic room in someone else's shabby home. She goes to public pools and Y's to clean up and, when she can get away with it, wash her clothes in the sinks. She is very lonely and sometimes tries to make conversation with other people at the pool. They are usually abrupt with her. Once when her overtures were rejected, she got so angry she deliberately urinated in the pool. Another time, she stole a towel to have something. It didn't help much. Though Jacquelyn's behavior was inappropriate, her anger was not. She is a human being and needs to be acknowledged.

It is easy to blame or laugh at isolates and escapists for self-destructive or socially unacceptable behavior. It is harder to ask about the sources of this behavior and try to remedy the problems. Like seekers and doctorers, isolates and escapists have unmet needs, which they try to meet as best as they can, alone. Nobody else will meet them or even notice that they exist.

CHAPTER TEN

Advocates and Assertive Older Women

THE SKILLS AND talents of older women are often employed or exploited in the service of various causes—political, environmental, feminist, educational, and others. Some of the women who work for these causes gain social status and a sense of identity and importance as advocates or community leaders. While some women are manipulated and others are given tedious chores and no power, the advocate role, like the volunteer route, sometimes leads to satisfaction or to a career. At any rate, it does allow for social interaction and sometimes for the ventilation of stockpiled hostility in an acceptable context.

What is often wasteful, however, is the fact that social services provided by older women advocates are usually offered on a precarious ad hoc basis. Many operate on grants or personal energies that run out before the task is completed.

If advocates eventually develop their own careers—with the contacts and experience they have gained—this is good for them but bad for the causes. Some women burn out and turn back to private life and commitments. It is easy to get discouraged, for advocacy is hard, and results are slow in coming. Ridicule eats away at the spirit. Yet more and more older Americans are recognizing their deprivation and becoming aware of the possibility of organizing as pressure groups. Older women, among the most discontent, are part of the movement.

Some assertive older women combine the advocate, nurturant, and career roles into a collective fight for their rights. Taking a cue from women's support and self-help groups, these older women nurture each other, fight sexism and ageism in the society and in themselves, advocate legislation and programs, and, in the process, perhaps, help the escapists, unutilized careerists, nurturers, isolates, faded beauties, doctorers, and seekers. They help by providing role models as well as by obtaining social innovations. Here are some examples.

Two Worcester, Massachusetts, women advocates, Kathleen Gooding and Jo Ann Bott, teamed up to start a number of projects to aid women. Kathleen, a black Quaker, originally from Trinidad, received her formal education late, starting at a Massachusetts two-year community college and eventually completing a master's degree at a university. Jo Ann, a white Presbyterian minister and psychologist, had been active in campus ministry and learned about the problems of many women. The two advocates organized a support group for women and a non-profit cooperative summer camp that offers women many opportunities for inexpensive weekends of growth, renewal, and relaxation. They have also started a year-round group residence for transitional women.

In Philadelphia, the International Society of Matrons, a black women's organization, worked with the Community College of Philadelphia to set up a program in which older persons of both sexes could get education late in life. Older women supplied the leadership for the organization.

Throughout the country, women have organized as advocates for battered wives and other victims. Older women can be, and often are, antennae sensing community needs and seeking ways to meet them on a personal or an organized level. It is largely older women who are the instigators of and volunteers in such programs as Meals on Wheels for the elderly and handicapped. As mentioned in the chapter on re-engaged nurturers, they are a source of labor and support in the insufficiently funded human services of our society. However, the advocacy and assertive role involves additional and somewhat different emotional elements than nurturant volunteering. Advocates and assertive older women have a sense of deprivation and a sense of entitlement;

they are determined to fight for their rights as individuals and collectives.

Assertiveness

It should be clear by now that assertion is not aggressive behavior. In contrast to aggression, assertion is not directed against another person but rather is an effort to obtain what one rightfully deserves in domestic, vocational, political, and other situations. In all these areas women have been taught to subordinate their needs to those of others, and that is why there has been such need for assertiveness training for women. Many women need to be resocialized before they can effectively work for equity.

Unfortunately not all those groups offering what they call assertiveness courses are disinterested. Like almost everything else in America, this training has become a business. Although many sincere people or organizations offer such courses for small fees, others charge as much as $300 for a several-day course of sometimes doubtful content and quality. It seems that whatever women do, they are subject to exploitation—because of their misery and unmet needs and, in some cases, because of their naiveté. Older women who have been taught to be trusting must learn to distrust and to be careful investigators of what is offered them in the name of the women's movement.

Older advocates also have to fight for fundamental rights against omnipresent prejudice and ridicule. It took from 1848 to 1920 to get women the right to vote; the fight for the Equal Rights Amendment is now entering its eighth discouraging year.

Backlash

Older women who are advocates are today in double jeopardy; the two backlashes are antifeminism and ageism. In triple jeopardy are the leftists among older women, for they are natural and vulnerable targets of the conservative reaction. It takes a great deal of strength to stand up to these pressures.

Sometimes assertive older women and advocates are successful in their battles for self or others and for social change. But often they lose, and this can be embittering and lead to withdrawal and anger—anger that can cause extreme depression when it goes unexpressed.

Dr. Janice W. Wetzel, University of Texas at Austin School of Social Work, reported in *Behavior Today* that women are significantly more at risk of depression than men. One out of five women suffers from clinical depressive symptoms, as compared to one out of every ten to fifteen males. Wetzel believes that the character traits that tend to correlate with depression are conscientiousness, social striving, relative inflexibility, submissiveness, and dependence. Advocates frequently seesaw between the traits she has identified. Advocates often work for causes and situations in which they believe themselves right, only to be slapped down. They then submit and seek approval in seemingly the only way open to them, a way in which they have been well schooled—humility. Secretly they are seething, however, and are unable to change their inward values.

As the backlash against women grows, many insecure older women are having a hard time adjusting. Their hopes were raised in the revolution of rising expectations. In the late sixties and early seventies it seemed as if there would be opportunity for them and their causes. Now, in a climate of conservatism and tax reduction, "good causes" and their advocates get axed. Certain liberal older women, once applauded for their leadership, are now an embarrassment to a society that does not want to know about human misery; it costs too much in money or social effort to help. Just as the older woman in Chapter 9 no longer dares collect for fund drives, many older women are afraid to espouse lost and losing liberal causes because they do not want to antagonize people. It is hard enough to be an older woman and so a general scapegoat anyway. It is often too much to bear to be a specific scapegoat for hostility in a society growing increasingly tense and acting out its frustrations. There is real fear in the eyes and voices of older women when they say such things as "I don't want them burning crosses on my lawn or making lampshades out of me." Older women know that inflation and alienation in Germany paved the way for Hitler, who targeted on intellectuals and liberals as well as Jews.

At the same time it is understandable that some older women, psychologically and economically squeezed, have themselves become advocates in the camp of the radical right. Accepted there, something for which older women are always grateful, they join and express their frustrations with a hostile collectivity that turns against welfare, government, minorities, and the poor. Feeling rejected by society, these women turn their anger against handy, though inappropriate, targets instead of the real sources of power and inequality. Such women occupy the front rows at protest meetings. Where else can they get a free seat? Their frustrations make them prey to the blandishments of demagogues. Glad to be needed, they work.

The following conversation between three women – one cashier and two customers – was overheard in a grocery store:

Woman 1 *(about 40): I can't believe the price of food. I feel like crying and walking out and not paying you, but my husband and I need to eat. By the time taxes are taken out of his salary, we have hardly anything, and after buying food, we have nothing.*

Woman 2 *(the cashier, about 40): I know. Do you think I like standing here all day in this noisy store? But we have two kids still at home and two in college, and we need my salary, lousy as it is. We can't get scholarships for them, or food stamps.*

Woman 3 *(about 50) chimes in: Well if you girls are smart, you'll do something about what is going on in this country. You will vote for conservative candidates who will stop welfare loafers. I am a widow who can't keep up her mortgage and taxes. I am collecting signatures for a man who says he will put a stop to it. Will you sign his papers so he can run?*

Agents or Victims of Change?

In times of tension, people become caught up in social currents. It feels better to be doing something than to be alone. If you are unemployed or underemployed, advocating for whatever cause is something to do. Identifying with the aggressor, even when the aggression is directed against your own kind or innocent others, seems safer than being isolated. Hampered by not having had much formal education, many older women today need to be very careful in weighing the information provided to them, especially since most of it comes from sources with vested interests of some sort. They need to ask whether they are being used or are the users.

To get their own rights and a good society, older women, like all Americans, need assertiveness and advocacy. The advocate role itself is appropriate. However, playing it out properly is not easy for anyone. It is especially hard for older women who must combat prejudice, lack of resources, education, their own timidity, and very difficult times. Women advocates can be change agents, but too often they also become change victims.

Women often want to change roles but are used to the old ones. When men refuse to change tires for them because women are "liberated," these women are victims because they don't yet know how to change tires. Moreover, it is hard to be persistent and flexible at the same time. Humor is a great help and a good weapon, but it is hard to laugh when you are hurting. And many older women and their causes are hurting badly today.

To become change agents without becoming change victims is a tightrope older women walk at ages when their acrobatic skills are usually waning. In fact, such women were never taught to be acrobats. They were taught to be honest, warm, helpful, compromising—not devious, withholding, adamant, or hostile. If they find themselves becoming angry, they feel guilty even if the hostility is well justified. They think they should understand and forgive and keep themselves in control even when mistreated.

Being human, they cannot always maintain control when slighted, but they suffer agonies of embarrassment when they explode. In addition, because women have long been characterized, in the media and sometimes in religion, as dirty and evil, they have internalized this cultural prejudice. They fear their impulses and, if they see themselves losing control, they panic. Unused to combat, they throw away their weapons and creep away.

Astrid had paid for a weekend at a beautiful mountain conference center a long ride from home in the hot city. On the first evening, she disagreed violently with a rabid speaker and said so during the discussion period. He became verbally abusive and she angrily replied in the same spirit. Suddenly, unused to such heated interchange, she had an overpowering feeling of hatred toward him. Instead of continuing the discussion or staying for the weekend for which she had paid, she threw her clothes into her suitcase and fled. It was nearly midnight, and she drove around for hours unable to find a room for the night. Finally, exhausted, she found a police station and asked permission to sleep in the parking lot in her car.

Besides fearing her own anger, Astrid, in typical female fashion, also felt betrayed because no one had come to her rescue when she was attacked. This lack of support is often the fate of no-longer-young women. One, for example, led a movement to get better pay for the lower-ranked employees in her social service organization, herself among them. When a new well-paid male director was to be brought in over the heads of others, she complained at a staff meeting. She was accused by a supervisor of "being resentful," which she had a right to be. Yet nobody defended her. This was so unpleasant that she learned painfully what the other women workers had already learned—rights-seeking is not always fruitful and is frequently punished. In fact, her situation at the agency became so uncomfortable that she started to look for another job, only to find them in short supply for older women. She continued working there but was even unhappier than before her revolt. She subsequently was given no raise in pay, and her professional mobility was blocked.

Unfortunately older women generally have few allies and little power. Coalitions are necessary for most power plays. Even younger women are not always sympathetic, a fact which has subjected the women's movement to some criticism, even from its supporters. Young women caught up in weighty problems of their own, often do not have the empathy, energy, or patience to deal with older women's issues. Moreover, younger women see older women as examples they do not wish to emulate in any way. It is easier to deny a dreaded future by looking the other way.

Moreover, though there are many of them, older women are not united, and they are certainly not homogeneous. Their cohort, economic, ethnic, and ideological differences divert them from such common grounds as their predominantly low status. Happy and successful older women, of whom there are many, do not always identify with their miserable sisters; they too may prefer to look away out of fear of their own futures. For safety, they often hide their own uncertainties and unhappinesses—from themselves and others.

Protected by being imbedded in families or jobs or with good finances women who are under less stress may feel that unhappy women are somehow at fault. As children, most women were taught that if they were "good girls" rewards would follow. Having reaped the rewards, some women feel entitled to them and do not understand that other women have had misfortunes not of their own making. In their desire to hold on to their good life, the fortunate tend, with some notable exceptions, not to get involved in attempts to organize or help unfortunate older women.

This general denial of the serious nature of older women's problems is especially strong because women, like men, almost universally deny that they are aging. Those aging are the *others*, not themselves. Richer women buy artifacts to conceal their age. They have no sympathy with grey hair—theirs being colored. They think women advocates would do better to use their energies improving their appearances. In fact, faded beauties are plainly bewildered that some women do not use cosmetics or color their hair. They consider them careless, lazy, stupid, or lesbians, though most are not.

Nurturer Laura, who told her story at the start of Chapter 1, listens avidly to the speeches of antifeminist Phyllis Schlafly. Although she does not belong to any antifeminist organizations, or any organizations except at her church, she agrees with everything Schlafly says. Partly this is because Laura is content and partly because, as a full-time, life-long nurturer, she does not like to believe that there may be better roles than the one she has lived. She needs to feel, as we all do, that our choices and lives are good. Laura thinks that out-of-home activities and agitation by women devalues and even undermines her own situation. Perhaps secretly she feels that being a grandmother is not quite enough but, if so, she probably believes, justifiably, that she has no good alternative and so had better be grateful for what she has. Laura says: "We women have it good; I don't know what troublemakers are complaining about."

Reactions to the Problem

It is likely that many older women, satisfied with their own situations or seeing no other option, may resent this book, which is, of course, my advocacy. There is some justification to this resentment. First, there is the tendency to blame the victim. Those who are already prejudiced against older women will use their problems to attack them. Secondly, there is the danger of reinforcing the unfortunate stereotypes of older women, already too prevalent in the society, by calling attention to the losers. I have not written here very much about the happy women who have good options. I have focused on those in a less happy situation because they are the ones who need attention and more oppotunities. Describing their misery may seem to indicate that to be aging and a woman is a guarantee of problems. Thus more denial and rejection sets in, and more stereotyping results.

These risks are run to call attention to the bad situation and lack of options many older women live with. Advocacy for and about them and by them is necessary. Assertiveness can be dangerous, but without it, and strong advocacy, there can be no improvement.

Ridiculed though they may be, older women must continue to press society about their oppression. Perhaps others will help them. One source of allies for women past their youth is an organization that is generally, but erroneously, considered to be exclusively for the more aged, those over 65. This is the Gray Panthers, whose slogan is "youth and age united" and which includes people of all ages, though the old predominate. A substantial number of women in their forties, fifties and sixties, and even younger, have found "a home" in this organization. They have become part of the "packs" (local chapters) and are active in the leadership of this militant, nonviolent group for social change. At the 1977 Chevy Chase, Md., convention such women were very prominent and very respected and welcomed. Issues of health service, housing, and income maintenance are as urgent for those under 65 as those over, and they are especially critical for women past their youth. Unlike other sectors in society, the Panthers do not reject mid-life women. The membership includes women like Alice Adler, a Chicago social worker and long-time activist, who is chairman of the Panthers thirty-person National Steering Committee. She arranged the first convention, in Chicago in 1975 and founded the lively Chicago Panthers. Billie Heller, wife of a Beverly Hills producer, comes from a consumer advocacy background and helped organize seven or eight Panther chapters in Los Angeles. Dr. Ellen Burns of the Catholic Social Service Center of Atlanta convened that city's interracial pack. A number of mid-life nuns are also active Panthers.

Capable Alice Adler is frequently mentioned as an understudy to Maggie Kuhn, Grey Panther founder. Although she vehemently denies this status, she does do a great deal of work for the national organization. The Panthers have a Task Force on Older Women.

At the Grey Panthers' 1977 National Convention, I participated in a stimulating session on older women. The fifty women
who participated ranged in age from the late teens to 80. Collec-
tively they came up with the following list of difficulties experienced by older women: depression, loneliness, income insecurity,
suicide, the embarrassment of outliving men, dependency and
forced independence, institutionalization, tranquilizers, nursing
homes, granny ghettos, fear of crime, bag ladies, redefining roles,
employment and transportation.

After writing these on the blackboard, the discussion leader,
Tish Sommers told them: "don't agonize, organize." And many
are. The organizations feminist older women and other advocates
are using are so many and varied that it would be inappropriate
and biased to present a limited listing here. But worth mention-
ing is the fact that at the 1977 meeting of the largest gerontological organization in America, the Gerontological Society, mid-life
women took leadership in setting up the National Action Forum
for Older Women. This group's purpose is to see that issues rele-
vant to older women get onto the programs of the Society's meetings. A network of advocates is being set up, and the advocates
are being instructed in the techniques of successful advocacy.

Partly as a result of nagging by women advocates, legislators
are becoming aware that older women hurt. Representative
Claude Pepper, Chairman of the House Select Committee on Aging, retained the services of a woman consultant, Ann Foote
Cahn, to prepare a hearing and publication on "American Women
in Mid-Life: Independence in Later Years."

The title is illustrative of government concern. As mentioned
in Chapter 1, the problems of older women have become troublesome to the society principally because of the costs government
incurs if these women are not able to support themselves. Limited
CETA retraining funds for displaced homemakers have come out
of recognition of the needs of older women pounded into the heads
of legislators by such tireless advocates as Tish Sommers, who
calls herself "a freelance agitator" but who was connected with

the Older Women's Task Force of NOW and the Alliance for Displaced Homemakers.

In the Alliance for Displaced Homemakers June 1978 report on national displaced-homemaker legislation, another displaced-homemaker advocate, National Coordinator Laurie Shields, provided some advice for older women advocates. She said, in what she called a "Dear Everyone Letter":

It's been quite a trip! A learning, caring, sharing experience that won't be shelved in a memory bank entitled "Past Pleasures." Instead, though the specific work of ADH might be over, we've only opened the door on the work that remains to be done. We won't bury the past—we'll build on it. We see six principles of action for older women:

1. Older women must build an advocacy base of our own. Consolidating the advances made through enactment of the displaced homemaker program, we've got to build a grassroots, organized force to attack other issues of special concern to older women.

2. We've got to continue the principle of focus. One issue at a time. DH movement won public support and official acceptance because it was zeroed in on a specific issue.

3. As older women, we must educate bureaucrats and the entire general public to the fact that older women have as much right to and need for a "fair share" of employment as other groups. Equal opportunity must not stop short at middle age.

4. As older women we must advocate for "paid peers." "Paid peers" —persons who have experienced a problem reaching out to assist others, promoting self-help instead of contained dependence on professional service delivery systems.

5. As older women we need to form partnerships at the local level with those in power. And, as a first individual step, we've got to learn to take our vested interests into the voting booth with us. We're used to speaking softly, now we have to learn the responsible use of the big stick—political clout.

6. As long as this society discounts the worth of its mothers and wives once their homemaking role within the family is ended, the ranks of displaced homemakers will grow. As older women we must tackle the cause of this disregard. THE HEART OF THE MATTER

IS RECOGNITION OF HOMEMAKING AS LEGITIMATE
LABOR AND MARRIAGE AS AN ECONOMIC PARTNERSHIP.

Shields' advice focuses on collective action, which is certainly
needed. It is also necessary and possible for older women to take
individual action when slighted, and older women are beginning
to do so with flair. Having the skills of survivorship, older women
with imaginations can be effective thorns in the flesh of their oppressors.

One woman, for example, blatantly discriminated against by
a bank because she was an older, and seemingly powerless older
woman, refused to turn her anger inward. She wrote a letter complaining of the discrimination. When she received a letter denying it and treating her like a stupid child, she figured out a way to
let the bank know that older women could retaliate. She withdrew from her checking account all funds but two cents. For several years now, the bank has been stuck with having to send her
monthly statements and yearly reports on the two cents. This has
cost the bank considerable postage and other expense. A number
of times the bank has begged the woman to close her account, but
each time she has responded by telling them she is leaving the
two cents there as a reminder to them to think twice before again
injuring an older woman.

Advocates are making some impact but they have a long,
hard road. Being an advocate is one role option for older women
and there are some good models available—though not enough.

Advice and Conclusion: Victims or Agents of Change?

SOME READERS may feel the picture of older women presented in this book will make women wish all the more not to grow old. Unfortunately the alternative to becoming older is not very good. Moreover, despite their miseries, most older women have satisfactions. The sun shines; flowers grow; trees and music are beautiful and so, sometimes, are memories and futures. Life, despite pain, is worth living. If they have nothing else, older women have themselves, and they are precious human beings.

There is also hope that things will improve. Women have strengths and they have renaissances. Older women too have a dream of being wanted and needed. That dream may be realized if more sympathy is aroused for them, and sincere attempts are made to include them in our ongoing society. Revised structures can facilitate this; human institutions are not carved in stone. They are habits of mind and interaction and can be changed with will and intelligence.

Humans have the capacity to redefine themselves and others. They can kill those they define as less than human, but they can also succor those they consider kin. Perhaps some day older women will be considered "we" instead of "they" or, worse still, "its."

Having separated the roles presently available to expose more clearly the reality for older women, let us now see how all the roles discussed can be drawn together positively and creatively.

For older women—in fact, for all humans—to fulfill themselves and improve the world, we must engage in enriched multiple roles. We should all nurture ourselves and others, cope with loss and re-engage, have friends and good leisure occupations, do meaningful and productive work as long as we are able and not at the whim of law or business, be eternally curious and learning seekers, be sufficiently narcissistic to respect and maintain the beauty of our bodies (including wrinkles), doctor ourselves intelligently as needed for physical and mental health, escape, retreat, and isolate ourselves enough to think, dream, and grow, and return to society with creativity and assertiveness to defend our own rights and those of others and to be advocates for equality, justice, and peace in the world.

Essentially, then, what the older woman needs is what all humans and societies need. What she gets, unfortunately, are very limited options. Like older men, older women suffer from the widespread faults of the society in general; unlike men, they suffer from the very particular twin evils of ageism *and* sexism.

In this book, I have tended to focus on unhappy older women because those are the ones who must be given better life chances. There are, of course, very many fulfilled older women, but there are not enough visibly happy ones to provide good role models for younger women. Innovative older women deserve more prominence and more of a chance to share their recipes for life. Perhaps there will be another book focusing on these, particularly successful and happy older women.

Older women are beginning to share. For example, some are now giving workshops on how to live communally instead of in isolation, how to become re-employed, how to go back to school, start businesses, etc. More cooperation and sharing are required, and we need to learn to share properly, not just for profit or as ego trips.

Communities need good places where both older women and men can discuss their common problems and join in pleasurable activities and meaningful endeavors. We must develop better ways to bring people together than the pitiful personal ads quoted in Chapter 9.

Older women do have to work at personal growth and advocacy and making good relationships. They must avoid excess self-pity, despite their deprivations. However, it is important to emphasize that the fate of women now old and those soon to be old does not rest largely in their own hands. Though individual actions can have some impact, it is more important to develop an overall social climate, social policy, and social concern. In the introductory chapter, Director Benedict of the Federal Administration on Aging was quoted as expressing concern that other priorities and the limitation of economic resources will prevent America from planning for an aging society. We need social arrangements, such as jobs, retraining, education, more recreational facilities, and new kinds of extended families to make it possible for older persons of both sexes to be integrated and valued in the society. Older people should be, in the words of Benedict, "considered a resource . . . to have responsibilities as well as rights." Robert Butler of the National Institute of Aging has expressed similar concerns.

As they increase in number, older women, and older men to a lesser extent, are in danger from a society that devalues them. Not only is it probable that they will not receive needed opportunities and social services, it is even possible that there will be sins of commission as well as omission. I have been frightened, at almost every meeting I attend on aging, to hear someone question whether it is really wise to give good preventive and medical attention to prolong life, since long livers are such burdens. Such a mentality is one step from the gas chambers and ice floes that have disposed of unwanted populations before in human history. As already noted, publicity about the troubles of the aging may de a disservice to them by providing ammunition for selfish and callous people who want to blame the victim. Actually, most older people of both sexes are healthy and competent; they give rather than receive. They would give more if they were allowed to.

A second danger, already mentioned in Chapter 10, is that

aware and militant older women will burn out when thwarted and frustrated in their efforts to help their peers and society. They deplete their own reserves of health and money, get exploited and emotionally drained and, too often, end up denigrated by themselves and others. They even, on occasion, turn on each other. Perhaps for this reason, I should have called this chapter "Never Pick Your Own Lilacs."

If you have a tiny lilac bush with only a few blossoms, the thing to do is to enjoy these flowers outdoors and hope the bush will grow. You can try to get a gift of lilacs from someone else's overgrown bushes, or you even "liberate" a few lilacs from bushes that are neglected, plentiful, and unnoticed.

Similarly, if you are a gardener in the very new older women's movement, you do not destroy the small growth with precipitous, opportunitistic plucking. You guard your first blooms. You do not tear down older women who have succeeded but admire them and hope success will be possible for more. You also educate them to help others. At the same time, you try to plant more bushes by working through the legislative process and pressuring and advocating assertively everywhere you can. You also water and fertilize, being very careful not to let yourself or others burn out or become such fanatics that you are unable to use tactics wisely or keep yourselves functioning and blooming for tomorrow. You put up fences where necessary. Women have been taught to be martyrs. Now they need to guard themselves, to stay strong, and to laugh more.

These are hard times for older women. But there are some opportunities, and some hopes. All we can do is try and attempt to have some joy while we are trying. At the end of the 1977 convention of the Gray Panthers, Maggie Kuhn gave the group a very serious charge to work for social change. But, she added, "never forget we are on a lark." I cannot add much to that good advice.

In trying to make a better world for themselves and others past youth, older women are really working for both sexes. We are all needy beings together in this world. We need each other!

Sadly, antagonisms have divided the sexes as women have

struggled to share equally in resources and power. Many men have also suffered from inequities and from some of our stupid and destructive social arrangements.

Older women's aspirations are for acceptance and activity within a caring context. Older women would like love, but they will settle for justice, amiability, and security. Is that not a minimum beginning for all humans everywhere?

Much of the responsibility for helping older women rests with the government. Mothers perform a valuable social function in producing socialized citizenry, and they are owed something better by society than they get. "Mom" has become a dirty word in our society because women cling too long to the only valued role many of them are ever given. This is a tragedy for everyone—not just the women. Should a mother with grown children be miserable because she cannot use her energies, she will not be a good spouse or mother of adults. If a widow or divorcée is unfulfilled, her children may be unresponsive to her needs, but her plight will nag at them. If they are over-responsive, they may become stunted in their own growth and lives. Seeing an unhappy older mother or never-married woman will make children phobic about getting old themselves, and they and young adults may avoid the sources of this phobia. In all, society loses.

For individuals, I offer some personal advice. Be aware that there are now few opportunities for older women in many places. Do not blame or despise yourself if you cannot fulfill your ambitions. Be openly angry, but do not brood. Remember, old chickens are tough; they survived the axe. Even bag ladies manage. Why not you? Take whatever opportunities *are* available and try to develop them and yourself. Get as much education as you can, either formally or informally. Ask other women for advice and also ask men. But don't be a dependent hypochondriac. Weigh advice carefully. Advice that belittles you, telling you to underrate yourself, is not good advice. Advice that unduly profits the giver or exploits you is also poor advice. Get real health care, not palliatives.

Also, do not abandon your ideals, but do recognize that

money is the medium of exchange in modern society. Expect fair pay for your work, and do not fall into the nurturance trap that you should give and give and never get. Not thanks but rather deprivation and corroding anger will be your reward if you do.

Older women have more beauty and ability than others recognize and more than they usually recognize themselves. You have experience and skills of survivorship from living long in a rough world. Figure out what your assets are and use them proudly. Be persistent about exploring resources in the community and avoid false pride. You are entitled to whatever limited help is available, even if it is given grudgingly.

It is not easy to cope with rejection. Perhaps it will be a bit easier if you understand that those doing the rejecting are scared of aging themselves and prejudiced against all older women, not you in particular. Perhaps they are projecting their own inadequacies or hatred of their mothers onto you. Above all, don't internalize their stereotypes. There is nothing wrong with you or most of your age-peers, but there is a good deal wrong with the cruel standards applied by an ageist, sexist society. Empathize with and aid those women who play out inappropriate roles; most of them have no good options. Help improve their options.

To carve out a new role in most environments is difficult. But the women who do so almost universally experience a resurgence of energy and accomplish a great deal for themselves and others. To change yourself and your situation late in life requires persistence, strength, and wisdom nobody should have to have at your age. But many other women are exhibiting amazing vitality these days. Please be a change agent, not a change victim.

Luck and opportunities are needed, along with support. Seek out friends and good role models. Cooperate with others to create sustaining structures. Share with others, including me, what you learn. If successful, become a role model for others.

Our daughters are coming, and all women are our daughters. What we do sets a new pattern for them and for the men coming, who are also our sons. Courage, my older sisters. You need it!

Sources and Resources

Anon. *An Annotated Bibliography on Woman and Aging*. Berkeley, Calif.: Interface Bibliographers, 1977. (Available from publisher at $3.00 per copy: 3018 Hillegass Ave., Berkeley 94705.)

Arieti, Silvano. "An Overview of Schizophrenia from a Predominantly Psychological Approach." *American Journal of Psychiatry*, March 1974, pp. 241-249.

Atchley, Robert. *The Social Forces in Later Life*. Belmont, Calif.: Wadsworth Publishing Co., Inc., 1972. Rev. ed. 1977.

Bart, Pauline. "Depression in Middle Aged Women." In *Growing Older*, edited by Margaret Hellie Huyck. Englewood Cliffs, N.J.: Prentice-Hall, 1974.

Bequaert, Lucia H. *Single Women: Alone and Together*. Boston: Beacon Press, 1977.

Berger, Bennet M. *Working Class Suburb: A Study of Auto Workers in Suburbia*. Berkeley and Los Angeles: University of California Press, 1977.

Block, Marilyn R., Davidson, Janice L., Grambs, Jean D., and Serock, Kathryn E. *Uncharted Territory: Issues and Concerns of Women over Forty*. College Park, Maryland: Center on Aging, University of Maryland, 1978.

Budapest, Z. *The Feminist Book of Light and Shadows*. Luna Publishers, 1976.

Butler, Robert N. *Why Survive? Being Old in America*. New York: Harper & Row, 1975.

California Department of Aging. *Age Discrimination in Employment*. Sacramento. (Available from 918 J. Street, Sacramento.)

Daniels, Arlene Kaplan. *A Survey of Research Concerns on Women's Issues*. Washington, D.C.: Association of American Colleges, 1975. (Available from AAC, 1818 R Street, NW, Washington, D.C.)

Davis, Audrey B. *Bibliography on Women: With Special Emphasis on Their Roles in Science and Society*. New York: Science History Publications, 1974. (Available from publisher, 156 Fifth Avenue, N.Y. 10010.)

Gans, Herbert. *The Urban Villagers*. Glencoe, N.Y.: Free Press, 1966.

Gerth, H. H., and Mills, C. Wright, eds. *From Max Weber: Essays in Sociology*. New York: Oxford University Press, 1956. (*See* especially "Science as a Vocation" and "Politics as a Vocation.")

164

Horner, Matina. "Fail Bright Women." In *Psychology Today*, November 1969.

Jacobs, Ruth Harriet. "Mobility Pains: A Family in Transition." *Family Coordinator*, April 1969, pp. 129-134.

————. "Passing Time." *Geriatric Digest*, May 1971.

————. "A Typology of Older American Women." *Social Policy*, December 1976, pp. 34-39.

Jacobs, Ruth Harriet, and Hess, Beth. "Panther Power: Symbol and Substance." *Long Term Care and Health Services Administration Quarterly*, Fall 1978, pp. 238-244.

Jacobs, Ruth Harriet, and Vinick, Barbara H. *Re-engagement in Later Life*. Stamford, Conn.: Greylock Press, 1979. Forthcoming.

Jaslow, Philip. "Employment, Retirement, and Morale Among Older Women." *Journal of Gerontology* 31 (1976): 212-218.

Kanter, Rosabeth Moss. *Men and Women*. New York: Basic Books, 1977.

Marshall, George N., and Poling, David. *Schweitzer: A Biography*. New York: Albert Schweitzer Fellowship, 1975.

Mead, George Herbert. *On Social Psychology: Selected Papers,* rev. ed. Chicago: University of Chicago Press, 1964.

Metropolitan Life Insurance Co. *Statistical Bulletin*, December 1977.

Miller, Jean Baker. *Toward a New Psychology of Women*. Boston: Beacon Press, 1977.

Mills, C. Wright. *The Sociological Imagination*. New York: Grove Press, 1961.

Morgan, Suzanne. "Sexuality After Hysterectomy and Castration." *Women and Health* 3 (January / February 1978): 5-10 (SUNY College at Old Westbury, N.Y. 11568)

Neugarten, Bernice L. *Middle-Aged and Aging*. Chicago: University of Chicago Press, 1968.

Neugarten, Bernice L., and Havighurst, Robert J., eds. *Social Policy, Social Ethics, and the Aging Society*. Report to the National Science Foundation. Washington, D.C.: U.S. Superintendent of Documents, 1976.

Portnoy, Frances. "What Keeps an Occupation in Its Place? A Case Study of Blocked Mobility in the Occupation of Nursing." Ph. D. dissertation, Brandeis University, 1975.

Sommers, Tish. "The Compounding Impact of Age on Sex: Another Dimension of the Double Standard." *Civil Rights Digest* 7 (1974): 3-9.

Sontag, Susan. "The Double Standard of Aging." *Saturday Review*, September 23, 1972, pp. 31-38. (Reprinted in Peter I. Rose, ed., *Seeing Ourselves*. New York: Knopf, 1975.)

Thomas, Lewis. "The Selves." *New England Journal of Medicine* 299 (July 1978): 185-186.

Toch, Hans. *The Social Psychology of Special Movements*. Indianapolis: Bobbs Merrill, 1965.

Troll, Lillian, Israel, Joan, and Israel, Kenneth. *Looking Ahead: A Woman's Guide to the Problems and Joys of Growing Older*. Englewood Cliffs, N.J.: Prentice-Hall, 1977.

U.S. Department of Commerce, Bureau of the Census. *Marital Status and Living Arrangements*. Current Population Reports. Washington, D.C., 1976.

U.S. Department of Commerce, Bureau of the Census. *Population Estimates and Projections*. Current Population Reports, Series P-25, no. 643. Washington, D.C., 1977.

U.S. Department of Commerce, Bureau of the Census. *A Statistical Portrait of Women in the United States*. Current Population Reports, Special Studies, Series P-23, no. 58. Washington, D.C., 1976.

U.S. Department of Health, Education and Welfare. *Facts about Older Americans*. Publication no. (OHDS) 79-20006. Washington, D.C., 1978.

U.S. Department of Labor. Bureau of Labor Statistics. *Mature Women Workers: A Profile*. Washington, D.C., 1976.

U.S. Department of Labor, Bureau of Labor Statistics. *Report 530: Where to Find BLS Statistics on Women*. Washington, D.C. (Single copies free.)

U.S. Department of Labor, Bureau of Labor Statistics. *Women in the Labor Force*. Washington, D.C., 1975.

U.S. Department of Labor, Women's Bureau. *The Earnings Gap Between Women and Men*. Washington, D.C., 1976.

U.S. House of Representatives, Select Committee on Aging. *Women in Midlife – Security and Fulfillment*, 2 vols. (Vol. 1, a compendium of papers; Vol. 2, an annotated bibliography). Washington, D.C.: Government Printing Office, 1979.

University of Michigan and Wayne State University Gerontology Centers. *The Older Woman in America*. 2 vols. Ann Arbor, 1974. (These volumes contain papers and notes from a conference held at the University of Michigan in 1973.)

Weideger, Paula. *Menstruation and Menopause*, rev. ed. New York: Delta Books 1977.

Wetzel, Janice R. Quoted in *Behavior Today*, April 24, 1978, p. 7.

Wheeler, Helen. *Womanhood Media: Current Resources About Women*. Metuchen, N.J.: Scarecrow Press, 1972.

Wilson, John. *Introduction to Social Movements*. New York: Basic Books, 1973.

Woolley, Sabra F. *Battered Women: A Summary*. Washington, D.C.: Women's Equity Action League, 1978. (Available from WEAL, 805 15th Street, NW, Washington, D.C. 20005 at $2.00 per copy.)

Young, Anne McDougall. *Going Back to School at 35 or Over*. Special Labor Force Report 204. Washington, D.C.: U.S. Department of Labor, Bureau of Labor Statistics, 1978.

INDEX